Professional SAS®
Programmer's Pocket Reference

Rick Aster

Windcrest®/McGraw-Hill

New York San Francisco Washington, D.C. Auckland Bogotá
Caracas Lisbon London Madrid Mexico City Milan
Montreal New Delhi San Juan Singapore
Sydney Tokyo Toronto

Editorial Consultant-Paul Nordquist

MS-DOS and Microsoft are registered trademarks and Windows is a trademark of Microsoft
    Corporation.
IBM and OS/2 are registered trademarks and System/370 is a trademark of International
    Business Machines Corporation.
SAS, SAS/ACCESS, SAS/AF, SAS/ASSIST, SAS/CPE, SAS/ETS, SAS/FSP, SAS/GRAPH,
    SAS/IML, SAS/OR, SAS/QC, SAS/SHARE, and SAS/STAT are registered trademarks and
    SAS/CALC, SAS/CONNECT, SAS/EIS, SAS/ENGLISH, SAS/INSIGHT, SAS/LAB,
    SAS/NVISION, SAS/PH-Clinical, and SAS/TOOLKIT are trademarks of SAS Institute Inc.
UNIX is a registered trademark of AT&T Information Systems.
VAX and VMS are trademarks of Digital Equipment Corporation.
Other product names that appear in this book are trademarks of their respective
    manufacturers.

Also by RICK ASTER

Professional SAS Programming Secrets (with Rhena Seidman) (Windcrest book No. 3612)
Professional SAS User Interfaces (Windcrest book No. 4083)
SAS System Primer: A Guided Tour For Decision-Makers (Windcrest book No. 4337)

FIRST EDITION
THIRD PRINTING

Library of Congress Cataloging-in-Publication Data

Aster, Rick.
     Professional SAS programmer's pocket reference / by Rick Aster.
        p.   cm.
     Includes index.
     ISBN 0-8306-4317-6 (p)
     1. SAS (Computer file)   I. Title.
     QA276.4.A83   1992
     519.5'028'55369—dc20   92-32890
                                                                      CIP

Editorial Director: Ron Powers
Book Editor: Andrew Yoder
Cover Design and Illustration: Sandra Blair Design, Harrisburg, Pa.

Contents

Preface

The SAS System is one of the largest pieces of software ever written. Because of its complexity, most of the books written about it — including those I've been involved with — have been large, heavy volumes. They have also been numerous — a shelf full of SAS books is a familiar sight wherever people use SAS software.

This book is different. It's comprehensive enough to serve as a primary reference source for any SAS programmer, but still small enough to carry around.

As this book took shape, I particularly remembered the people who travel with the SAS System on portable computers. Here, finally, is a reference book you'll want to take with you.

If you are just starting out and want to learn SAS programming the quick way, use the reference material in this book to illuminate your experimentation with the SAS System, in combination with a book that teaches SAS programming concepts and techniques, such as *Professional SAS Programming Secrets* by Rick Aster and Rhena Seidman (Windcrest/McGraw-Hill book 3612).

1

Introduction to SAS software

Being a SAS programmer means working with the SAS System. Most of the SAS language features described in this book relate to particular aspects of the SAS System.

The SAS System

The SAS System is a set of related programs for working with data. It is one of the largest and most widely used integrated software systems. Although it covers a broad range of computer applications, it is best known for its capabilities in managing, analyzing, and presenting data. Most of the work that people do with the SAS System combines these three processes.

The SAS System is published by SAS Institute Inc., and it consists of over a dozen separate products. This book focuses primarily on base SAS software, which is the central part of the system. The different SAS products are described in chapter 19.

The SAS language

The SAS language is a general-purpose high-level programming language that you use to call upon the different capabilities of the SAS System. The SAS language compares to Fortran, PL/1, and C, but it also has some unique features that affect the way you program with it.

A SAS program is divided into steps, which run independently in sequence, one after another. The two kinds of steps are *data steps* and *proc steps*. Steps and programming are described in chapter 2. The general rules of SAS syntax are covered in chapter 3. The rest of the book supplies the specific details.

SAS datasets

The most important special feature of the SAS language is its built-in support for the SAS System's file types. The main kind of SAS file is the *SAS dataset*.

A SAS dataset stores data in table format, with the rows of the table treated as observations and columns as variables. Each observation in a SAS dataset contains a value for each variable in the SAS dataset. There can be any number of observations. Usually, there are only a few variables.

The header, a separate block of data at the beginning of the SAS dataset, contains general information about the SAS dataset. Most importantly, it contains the name of each variable in the SAS dataset and other attributes of the variables.

In SAS programming, all SAS datasets can be treated conceptually as having the same general shape — even though the physical form in which some SAS datasets are stored is completely different. With the SAS language's high-level support for SAS datasets, you can use a SAS dataset in a SAS program without having to be concerned with the specific details of the way the data is stored.

SAS datasets and other SAS files are described in chapter 11.

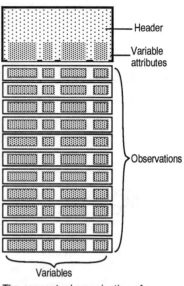

The conceptual organization of a SAS dataset.

I/O

File input and output, or I/O, is part of every SAS program. The SAS language, in effect, supports two I/O systems: a simplified one for SAS datasets and a more flexible one for other files, which are treated as text files whether or not they actually contain text. SAS text file handling is among the most powerful and capable of any programming language.

In SAS programs, SAS files and text files are not usually known by the physical names that the computer's operating system assigns. Instead, they are known by librefs and filerefs, which are names that the SAS System defines. The LIBNAME and FILENAME statements, described in chapter 4, are used to associate physical file names with librefs and filerefs.

A libref identifies a SAS data library, which can contain one or more SAS datasets or other SAS files. The SAS files in a library are called *members*. A SAS file is identified by a two-level name, combining the libref and member name. For example, WORK.LIST is a SAS file LIST in the WORK library.

Routines

The SAS System contains six essential kinds of routines that you can use in a SAS program: procs, engines, functions, CALL routines, informats, and formats. Each kind of routine is described briefly here. The routines themselves are covered in the later chapters of this book.

Procs

Procs, or *procedures,* are specialized applications programs that do a wide range of things. You use a proc in a separate step of a SAS program.

Engines

Engines mediate access to SAS files. You rarely have to think about engines; in most SAS work, you can just use the defaults.

Functions

Functions are used to build expressions — usually mathematical expressions, to calculate a value based on one or more other values.

CALL routines

CALL routines are simple subprograms that are used in the CALL statement.

Informats

Informats are used to convert text data to other kinds of data, especially when reading text files.

Formats

A *format* converts a specific kind of data to text. Formats are used especially when writing text files.

SAS session

A *SAS session* begins when you issue a command to the operating system to launch the SAS System. The exact form of the command depends on what operating system you are using and how the SAS System is installed. Often, however, the command is simply:

sas

or "SAS" followed by a release number, such as:

sas607

In a windowing operating environment with icons and menus, you open the SAS System the same way you open other applications.

In a SAS session, you can run one or more SAS programs. Display manager, the default mode of a SAS session, uses different windows to provide different points of view on the SAS session. To run a SAS program, you use the program editor window. First, type the program in the program editor window, or import it using a command, such as the INCLUDE command. Then, enter the SUBMIT command to execute the program. Results appear in the log and output windows. If necessary, you can retrieve the submitted program using the RECALL command. Then, you can revise the program and run it again.

INCLUDE, SUBMIT, and RECALL are just a few of the many commands that can be used in a display manager session, and the program editor window is just one of many windows. Display manager windows and commands are described in chapter 13.

Most operating systems support other modes for SAS sessions. One such mode is noninteractive mode, which runs a single SAS program without providing access to other SAS System features. Interactive line mode is an old-fashioned line-mode style with no windows or commands. System options that are in effect when you launch the SAS System determine what mode a session uses.

Some SAS language features can be used only in certain modes. The restricted use of those features is indicated in this book with a note like this one: **Mode** Display manager.

System options allow you to change the way a SAS session operates. They can be set when you start a session; most can also be changed in the middle of a session. System options are described in chapter 9.

Several libraries are automatically present in every SAS session. The most important is the WORK library, which SAS programmers usually use for storing SAS files temporarily during a session. The WORK library and other automatic libraries are described in chapter 11.

An interactive session continues until you do something to end it. You can end the session with the ENDSAS statement or with a command.

Batch

Batch mode, a feature of larger operating systems, allows the operating system to determine the schedule of programs. Programs that are run in batch mode cannot have any user interaction.

Automatic print files

Two print files are automatically present in every SAS session to hold print output from programs.

Log

The *log* contains the program lines of SAS programs you run, messages about the programs, and output from some procs and data steps. If a SAS program you submit is written incorrectly, you can expect the log to contain informative error or warning messages. You can use system options to control the kinds of things that are displayed in the log. In a display manager session, the log appears in the LOG window. In a SAS program, the log is known by the fileref LOG.

Standard print file

The *standard print file* contains print output from most procs and some data steps. In a display manager session, the standard print file appears in the output window. In a SAS program, the standard print file is known by the fileref PRINT.

Implementations

The SAS System is not a single, static product, so the SAS language is not always exactly the same. The SAS System changes from year to year with new releases and revisions. It also varies to take advantage of special features of the different operating systems that it runs on.

Major features that are not supported by all recent releases and all current operating systems are identified with this kind of note: **Operating system** Microsoft Windows **Release** 6.07+. The feature is mostly supported by the release indicated number, and should be fully supported by later release numbers. It might also be partly supported by the previous release number. *Multiuser* refers to operating systems that run primarily on computers with several users; *Single-user* refers to those that run primarily on computers with only one user, including UNIX.

Notation

Syntax entries in this book use these notational conventions:

CODE FONT	use these characters as shown
italic terms	substitute appropriate values
or	alternatives; use one
. . .	pattern can continue, or additional terms allowed
options */ options* *optional* *(options)*	these terms can be omitted
'text'	character constant
n	whole-number constant
item list	one or more items, separated by blanks
=(list)	omit parentheses if there is only one item

2

Programming

A SAS program is made up of data steps, proc steps, and global statements, which can be put together in any order. Global statements usually control parameters or characteristics of the SAS session. Steps usually do something with data.

Steps

Steps are a distinctive feature of the SAS language. A program can contain any number of steps. The steps are executed in the order in which they appear in the program. Often, the first step in a program creates a SAS dataset, and subsequent steps analyze the SAS dataset and produce reports.

A step can be either a data step or a proc step. A data step does whatever you program it to do. Data steps are most often used to create SAS datasets. A proc step runs a SAS proc. The results of a proc step depend on what proc is run and how it is used.

A step consists of several statements. In some cases, a proc step might consist of only one statement.

Data step programming

The data step is what makes the SAS language a general programming language. In a data step, you can creates variables, compute values, and work with files. A data step can include control flow statements to allow programming of any degree of complexity. But the data step was invented to create SAS datasets, and that is what it is usually used to do.

The first statement in a data step is a DATA statement, which names the SAS datasets that the step creates. After the DATA statement, there are two main kinds of statements: *executable* statements and *declaration* (or *nonexecutable*) statements. Executable statements spell out events that actually occur when the data step runs. The order of the statements is important. Declaration statements usually define characteristics of variables that appear in the step. The order of declaration statements is less important, although some declaration statements have to come before executable statements that use the same variables. Often, programmers put all the declaration statements at the beginning of the step, right after the DATA statement.

The data that forms a SAS dataset has to come from somewhere. It could be extracted from a text file or one or more SAS datasets. It could be entered by the user in a window that is displayed by the DISPLAY statement. Or, with the use of the INPUT and CARDS statements, it could be right there in the SAS program itself. This is an example of a data step that creates a SAS dataset from data lines in the program file:

```
DATA WORK.HOWIE;
  LENGTH POST $ 3;
  INFILE CARDS;
  INPUT POST NUMBER AMOUNT;
CARDS;
AAA 123 123
BBB 123 123
CCC 132 321
DDD 440 040
EEE 140 150
FFF 180 198
;
```

This data step creates the SAS dataset WORK.HOWIE, as indicated in the DATA statement. The LENGTH statement declares the variable POST as a character variable of length 3. Variables in data steps do not have to be declared, but declaring a character variable ensures that the variable will be the right length. The INFILE statement indicates that the INPUT statement will read from CARDS, that is, the data lines following the CARDS statement. The INPUT statement reads the variables POST, NUMBER, and AMOUNT from the data lines. Because NUMBER and AMOUNT have not been declared, they are numeric variables. The CARDS statement marks the end of the data step and the beginning of the data lines.

The statements in the data step execute repeatedly as long as there is more input data. The automatic loop in a data step is called the *observation loop*. Each time the bottom of the data step is reached, an observation is automatically written to the output SAS dataset. The SAS dataset includes all three of the variables in the data step. Because there are six input lines, the SAS dataset is created with six observations.

The data step can be modified to introduce these common variations:

• Using an INFILE statement with the fileref of an input text file in order to read data from a separate file.
• Using informats and pointer controls in the INPUT statement for formatted input.
• Additional programming statements to create additional variables or to recode variables.
• A subsetting IF statement to select parts of the input data with a particular characteristic.

- One or more PUT statements to write messages in the log.
- PUT statements together with a FILE statement to produce an output text file or print file.
- Dataset options in the DATA statement to alter the way that the output SAS dataset is written, such as the KEEP= dataset option to select variables to be stored in the SAS dataset, or the COMPRESS= option to control whether the SAS dataset is stored in compressed format.
- FORMAT, LABEL, and other statements to set the attributes of the variables in the step. The variable attributes in the data step are also stored in the output SAS dataset.
- Creating two or more SAS datasets, with OUTPUT statements and control flow statements to determine which observation are written to which output SAS datasets. When a data step contains OUTPUT statements, observations are written only when an OUTPUT statement is executed.
- Creating two or more SAS datasets with the same observations, but with different sets of variables, according to the KEEP= dataset option in the DATA statement.
- A data step with no output SAS dataset, using the DATA _NULL_ statement.
- Instead of an INPUT statement, data entered by the user in a window displayed by the DISPLAY statement.
- An INPUT statement used together with a DISPLAY statement to allow the user to modify data read from a text file.
- Data read from an input SAS dataset using a SET statement.
- Data read from a combination of two or more SAS datasets in a MERGE or SET statement.
- Dataset options used on the input SAS datasets, such as the OBS= option to limit the number of observation read from a SAS dataset.
- A data step with no input data. When there is no input data, there is no automatic loop, and the data step stops when the last statement or a RETURN statement is reached.

Control flow statements, such as IF . . . THEN and GOTO, can be used to control the order in which executable statements are executed. Declaration statements are not affected by control flow statements.

Statement labels are used by some control flow statements. With a few exceptions, any statement in a data step can have a statement label, although statement labels only really have to do with the executable statements. A statement label is a name that comes before the statement and is followed by a colon, as in this example:

HERE: INPUT POST NUMBER AMOUNT;

Each step in a program is independent, so the control flow statements of one data step have no effect on any other data step.

Examples

This data step creates a SAS dataset from data entered in a data entry window:

```
DATA NEW;
  WINDOW LIST #1 @4 'Enter data or END command.'
    #4 @4 'Country' +1 COUNTRY $CHAR32.
    #5 @4 'Year' +1 YEAR 4.;
  DISPLAY LIST;
RUN;
```

This data step creates a SAS dataset that contains some observations from another SAS dataset:

```
DATA FREEZE;
  SET WEATHER;
  IF TEMP < 0;
RUN;
```

Proc step programming

A *proc step* runs a SAS proc. Most procs are versatile, and you control their behavior by the options and statements you supply in the proc step.

The first statement of a proc step is the PROC statement, which begins by identifying the proc that is being run. For a few procs, that's all the proc step has to be. For example, to run the OPTIONS proc, you can just use this statement:

```
PROC OPTIONS;
```

Most procs use input data from a SAS dataset, which you identify using the DATA= option in the PROC statement. For example, to print the SAS dataset WORK.CALLEY, you can use the PRINT proc, beginning with this statement:

```
PROC PRINT DATA=WORK.CALLEY;
```

The DATA= option is just one of many options you can use on the PROC PRINT statement. Each proc has its own set of options for the PROC statement.

Most procs also use additional statements. In the PRINT proc, for example, you can use the VAR statement to list the variables to be printed. The syntax of statements is different for each proc. However, there are some statements that work the same way in most procs. The BY statement, for example, can be used in most procs to form observations in the input SAS dataset into groups.

The RUN statement can usually be used to mark the end of a proc step. The proc step begins running only when the end of the step is reached. However, some procs can run in segments, a few statements at a

time. The group of statements that run at one time is called a *run group*.
In run-group procs, the RUN statement marks the end of the run group,
but not necessarily the end of the proc. You can use the QUIT statement
to mark the end of those procs.

Examples

These steps sort a SAS dataset, change some of its variable names, then
print it:

```
 PROC SORT DATA=HOME.EXTENT;
   BY DATE;
RUN;

 PROC DATASETS LIBRARY=HOME;
   MODIFY EXTENT;
   RENAME STRY=STORIES  AR=AREA;
QUIT;

 PROC PRINT DATA=HOME.EXTENT;
   ID DATE;
   FORMAT DATE YYMMDD8.  AREA COMMA7.;
RUN;
```

3

General rules

Some general rules create the characteristic "look" of the SAS language. These rules apply to all statements throughout any SAS program.

Tokens and spacing

A program is made of meaningful units called *tokens*. Most tokens are either words, consisting of letters and perhaps digits, or symbols, consisting of one or more special characters. Constants are a separate kind of token.

A space is required between two consecutive tokens, unless either of the tokens is a symbol. Any number of spaces and line breaks can appear between any two tokens. Spaces cannot be added between the characters that make up a token, except for some symbols and compound words.

Uppercase letters and lowercase letters are equivalent to each other and can be used interchangeably.

Comments

A *comment* can be delimited by the symbols /* and */ and can appear between any two tokens. Alternatively, you can use a comment statement, which begins with an asterisk (*). A comment statement can appear between any two statements.

Statements

A program is made up of *statements*. A semicolon (;) marks the end of each statement. The first token in a statement is usually a keyword that is the name of the statement. A few statements, especially the assignment statement, do not begin with a keyword.

Names

Various objects in SAS programs are given *names*. These SAS names can be up to eight characters long. The first character must be a letter or underscore. Subsequent characters can be letters, underscores, and digits.

These SAS naming rules apply to variables, arrays, statement labels, SAS datasets, librefs, filerefs, and other objects. Additional restrictions apply to the names of some objects.

A list of names is formed using spaces as separators. These forms of abbreviated lists can also be used in some statements:

NAME1-NAME5	NAME1 NAME2 NAME3 NAME4 NAME5
NAME08-NAME10	NAME08 NAME09 NAME10
ALL	All
CHARACTER *or* _CHAR_	All character variables
NUMERIC	All numeric variables
FROM--TO	A range of consecutive variables
FROM-NUMERIC-TO	Numeric variables in a range
FROM-CHARACTER-TO	Character variables in a range
FROM-CHAR-TO	

4

Global statements

Global statements are executed between steps in a SAS program. If they appear before the end of a step, they are executed before the step is executed.

The %INCLUDE, %LIST, %PUT, and %RUN statements were formerly global statements, but are now implemented as macro statements. They are described in chapter 10.

*

* text;   Comment statement: not executed as part of program.

DM

DM '*display manager commands*' *option*;   DM *window* '*commands*' *option*;
Executes the display manager commands. If a window is named, commands are executed for that window. **Mode** Display manager

Option

CONTINUE   If the commands activate a window, this option activates that window again after all submitted statements are executed. **Release** 6.07+

Example
DM 'CLEAR LOG; CLEAR OUTPUT';

ENDSAS

ENDSAS;   Ends the SAS session.

FILENAME

FILENAME *fileref optional device* '*physical file or directory name*' *options*;
Associates the fileref with the physical file name.

FILENAME *fileref device options*;   Associates the fileref with the device.

FILENAME *fileref or* _ALL_ CLEAR;   Clears the fileref.

FILENAME *fileref or* _ALL_ LIST;   Lists information about the fileref in the log.

Options

BLKSIZE *or* BLK=*n* LINESIZE *or* LS=*n* LRECL=*n* RECFM=D *or* F *or* N *or* P *or* U *or* V MOD NEW OLD PAGESIZE *or* PS=*n*

For named pipes: BLOCK *or* NOBLOCK BYTE *or* MESSAGE EOFCONNECT RETRY=*time* SERVER *or* CLIENT **Operating system** OS/2

For DDE: HOTLINK NOTAB **Operating system** OS/2

DISP= SPACE= VOLSER *or* VOL= UNIT= LABEL= NOMOUNT REUSE
BUFNO=*n* DSORG= OPTCD= **Operating system** MVS

UNBUF **Operating system** UNIX

ALQ=*n* CC=FORTRAN *or* PRINT *or* CR DEQ=*n* FAC=(DEL, GET, PUT, UPD)
KEY= KEYVALUE > *or* >= *or* < *or* <= *value* MBC=*n* MBF=*n*
SHR=(DEL, GET, PUT, UPD, NONE) **Operating system** VMS

Example
FILENAME RES 'SYS.RES';

FOOTNOTE

FOOTNOTE*n* '*text*' ... ; $1 \le n \le 10$ Sets the specified footnote line to the
text string specified. Resets all higher-numbered footnote lines.

FOOTNOTE*n*; $1 \le n \le 10$ Resets the footnote line and all higher-
numbered footnote lines.

LIBNAME

LIBNAME *libref optional engine* '*physical file name*' *options*;   Associates
the libref with the physical file name.

LIBNAME *libref or* _ALL_ CLEAR;   Clears the libref.

LIBNAME *libref or* _ALL_ LIST;   Lists information about the libref in the
log.

Options

ACCESS=READONLY Read-only. ACCESS=TEMP Scratch. **Release** 6.07+

DISP= SPACE= VOLSER *or* VOL= UNIT= BLKSIZE=*n* **Operating system**
MVS

ALQ=*n* BKS=*n* BUFSIZE=*n* CACHESIZ=*n* DEQ=*n* MBF=*n* **Operating system**
VMS

Examples
LIBNAME MAX 'NEWSMAX.SDL';
LIBNAME MAX CLEAR;

LOCK

LOCK *libref or SAS file or entry option*;   Locks the file.

LOCK *libref or SAS file or entry* CLEAR;   Unlocks the file.

LOCK *libref or SAS file or entry* LIST;   States in the log whether the file is
locked.

Release 6.07+

MISSING

MISSING *characters*;   *characters*: A, a, B, b, . . . , _   Allows the specified
characters to be read as special missing values by most numeric informats.

Example
MISSING L X l x;

Null

;   No effect.

OPTIONS

OPTIONS *system options*;   Sets the values of system options.
Alias OPTION

Example

OPTIONS COMPRESS=NO NODATE PAGENO=1;

PAGE

PAGE;   Starts a new page in the log.

SKIP

SKIP;   Skips a line in the log.

SKIP *n*;   Skips *n* lines in the log.

TITLE

TITLE*n* '*text*' ... ; $1 \le n \le 10$ Sets the specified title line to the text string specified. Resets all higher-numbered title lines.

TITLE*n*; $1 \le n \le 10$ Resets the title line and all higher-numbered title lines.

Example

TITLE1 'Saturday Morning';

TSO

TSO '*command*';   Executes the TSO command.

TSO;   Temporarily exits to TSO.

Operating system/Mode Ignored except under MVS/TSO

X

X '*command*';   Executes the operating system command.

X;   Temporarily exits to operating system shell.

Mode Ignored in batch mode in some operating systems

5

Data step statements

The DATA statement marks the beginning of a data step. A CARDS, CARDS4, or RUN statement, if present, marks the end of the data step. Otherwise, the end of the step is the beginning of the next step or the end of the SAS session.

A RETURN statement is implied at the end of every data step. Except after a LINK statement, a RETURN statement includes the effect of an OUTPUT or UPDATE statement if the step does not contain an OUTPUT, UPDATE, or REMOVE statement.

Most data step statements are executable statements, representing actions that occur when the step is run. Others are declaration statements. Declaration statements that relate to input or output SAS datasets can be placed anywhere in the step. Declaration statements that relate to data step variables should usually appear before executable statements that refer to the same variables.

The few other data step statements can be used only in particular spots in the data step. A data step can also contain global statements, which are executed before the data step.

Executable, declaration, and global statements can have statement labels, but statement labels are only really meaningful in reference to executable statements.

In the entries that follow, these symbols identify the different kinds of statements:

≡	executable
66	declaration
{ }	beginning/ending of step
◆	restricted

ABORT

ABORT *options*; ≡ Stops execution of the data step and the SAS program.

Options RETURN ABEND *n* Effects vary by operating system.

ARRAY

ARRAY *array* {*subscript range*, . . .} *optional length or* $ *length optional variable list or* _TEMPORARY_ / *optional* (*initial value*, . . .); 66 Declares an explicitly subscripted array, using the variables listed as elements of the array. If no variables are listed, variable names are constructed by appending 1, 2, 3, etc., to the array name. The keyword _TEMPORARY_ can be used for an array of temporary variables. All of the elements must be of the same type. If a length term is used, it sets the length for any variables created by the ARRAY statement. For a one-dimensional array, the subscript range can be one of the following:

n   subscripts from 1 through *n*

n:n   subscripts that cover the indicated range

★   subscripts from 1 through the number of variables listed

For a multidimensional array, the subscript range can be *n* or *n:n* for each dimension. The subscript range must match the number of variables listed as elements. Initial values can optionally be provided for all the elements in the array.

ARRAY *array* (*optional index variable*) *variable list*;   "   Declares an implicitly subscripted array, using the variables listed as the elements of the array. All the elements must be of the same type.

Example
ARRAY MSB{3, 5} $ 6 MSB1-MSB-15;

Assignment

variable = *expression*;   ≡   Assigns the value of the expression to the variable. If the type of the expression is different from the type of the variable, an automatic type conversion is done.

SUBSTR(*character variable, position, optional length*) = *expression*;   ≡ Assigns the value of the expression to the segment of the indicated character variable.

Examples
DF = DC★1.8 + 32;

WORD = 'now';
SUBSTR(WORD, 2, 1) = 'e';   ★ Changes WORD to "new";

ATTRIB

ATTRIB *variable attributes*;   "   Declares one or more attributes for a variable. Attributes can be one or more of the following:

LENGTH=*n or* LENGTH=$ *n*   The length of the variable, in bytes. Use $ for a character variable.

INFORMAT=*informat specification*

FORMAT=*format specification*

LABEL='*label*'   A descriptive phrase that can be up to 40 characters long.

BY

BY *sort order option*;   ◆   Indicates that the input SAS dataset(s) is (are) sorted or grouped by the indicated variables. Creates the automatic FIRST. and LAST. variables for each BY variable. Used only immediately after a SET, MERGE, MODIFY, or UPDATE statement.

Sort order

The sort order clause consists of one or more of the following:

variable Sorted in ascending order by this variable.

DESCENDING *variable* Sorted in descending order by this variable.

Option

NOTSORTED The input data is grouped but not necessarily sorted.

CALL

CALL *routine(arguments)*; ≡ Executes the CALL routine.

CARDS

CARDS; DATALINES; } Marks the end of the step and the beginning of data lines. Data lines continue until a line that contains a semicolon is reached:

CARDS;
data lines
;

CARDS PGM=*name*; } Compiles the step. The compiled step, when run, will read from data lines that follow the RUN statement. **Release** 6.03–6.07

CARDS4

CARDS4; DATALINES4; CARDS4 PGM=*name*; } The same as the CARDS statement, except that a semicolon does not mark the end of the data lines. Data lines continue up to a line of four semicolons:

CARDS4;
data lines
;;;;

CONTINUE

CONTINUE; ≡ Branches to the bottom of the (innermost) DO loop. Use only in a DO loop. **Release** 6.07+

DATA

DATA *SAS datasets or* _NULL_ / *option*; { Names all output SAS datasets of the data step.

DATA; { The same as DATA _DATA_; .

DATA PGM=*compiled data step*; { Identifies a compiled data step to be run.

Options

PGM=*SAS file* Compiles the data step and stores it in the file named. **Release** 6.07+

VIEW=*SAS dataset* Creates a view from the data step and stores it in the SAS dataset named. The SAS dataset must be one of the output SAS datasets named in the DATA statement. **Release** 6.07+

DELETE

DELETE; ≡ Stops execution of the current repetition of the observation loop; branches to the top of the observation loop.

DISPLAY

DISPLAY *window or window.group options*; ≡ Displays a window that is defined in the WINDOW statement. If a group is specified, the fields in that group are displayed. The window remains displayed until the the data step ends. The user can enter the END command in the window to stop execution of the data step.

If the automatic variable _MSG_ has a value, that value is displayed in the message line of the window. If the user enters a command that is not recognized as a display manager command, the command line is assigned to the automatic variable _CMD_. **Mode** Display manager

Options

BLANK Previously displayed fields in the window are erased.

NOINPUT Does not allow user input.

BELL Beeps.

Example

```
DATA _NULL_;
  WINDOW GREETING
    #7 @9 'This is a data step window'
    #9 @9 'Press enter to continue';
  DISPLAY GREETING BLANK;
  STOP;
RUN;
```

DO

DO; *statements* END; ≡ Forms a simple block. A block is treated as a unit for control flow purposes.

DO *iteration control*; *statements* END; ≡ Forms a loop. The statements in the loop execute repeatedly until a stopping condition is reached. The iteration control can be one or more of the following:

numeric variable = *start* TO *stop* optional BY *increment* The numeric variable is set to the start value. The increment value, or the default 1, is added whenever the bottom of the loop is reached. The loop stops when the value of the variable passes the stop value.

WHILE(*condition*) The loop stops if the condition is false.

UNTIL(*condition*) The loop stops after the first time through if the condition is true.

DO OVER *implicitly subscripted array*; *statements* END; ≡ Forms a loop. The statements in the loop execute repeatedly, once for each element of the array.

Example

```
DO I = 1 TO 8;
  SQUARE = I*I;
  PUT I= SQUARE=;
  END;
```

DROP

DROP *variable list*; **"** Equivalent to the DROP= dataset option for all
output SAS datasets in the step. If the KEEP= or DROP= dataset option is
also used on an output SAS dataset, the DROP statement is applied first.

ELSE

ELSE *action* ◆ Immediately following an IF . . . THEN statement, it
executes the action if the condition in the IF . . . THEN statement is false.

END

END; ◆ Marks the end of a block.

ERROR

ERROR . . . ; ≡ Sets the value of the automatic variable _ERROR_ to 1.
Additional terms can be used in the statement, as in the PUT statement, to
write a message to the log.

FILE

FILE *fileref or 'physical file name' options*; ≡ Sets the current output
text file to the file indicated.

Options

PRINT A print file. NOPRINT A nonprint file.

RECFM= Record format. Values vary by operating system.
F Fixed length. V Variable length. U Undefined. D Data sensitive.
N No format. P Print format.

LRECL=*n* Logical record length: the number of characters in a record.

PAD Pads short records (shorter than the logical record length) with trailing blanks. This is the default for fixed-length records. NOPAD Does not
pad with trailing blanks. This is the default for variable-length records.

LINESIZE *or* LS=*n* Line size: the maximum number of characters that can
be written to a record.

OLD Starts writing records at the beginning of the file.
MOD Starts writing records at the end of the file.

NOTITLES NOTITLE Title lines and footnote lines are not written on each
page of output.

N=*n or* PAGESIZE *or* PS The number of lines that are available to the
output pointer. For a print file, the only values allowed are 1 or PAGESIZE
or PS.

PAGESIZE *or* PS=*n* Page size: the number of lines on a page. Overrides
the system option of the same name.

HEADER=*statement label* When a PUT statement writes the end of a page
in the file, it branches to the statement label to execute a group of
statements there until a RETURN statement is reached. Control then
returns to the PUT statement.

COLUMN *or* COL=*variable* A numeric variable that the PUT statement sets
to the column pointer location.

LINE=*variable* A numeric variable that the PUT statement sets to the line pointer location.

LINESLEFT *or* LL=*variable* A numeric variable that shows the number of lines left on the page, including the current line pointer location.

FILENAME=*variable* A character variable that shows the physical name of the file. **Release** 6.06+

FILEVAR=*variable* A character variable that can be used to change the physical output file. Changing the value of the variable causes the FILE statement to close the input file and open the file whose physical name is the value of the variable. **Release** 6.06+

BLKSIZE=*n* BLK=*n*

CCHHR=*variable* CLOSE=*position* DCB=*fileref* DEVTYPE=*variable*
DSCB=*variable* JFCB=*variable* UCBNAME=*variable* VOL=*variable*
Operating system MVS

For named pipes: BLOCK *or* NOBLOCK BYTE *or* MESSAGE EOFCONNECT
RETRY=*time* SERVER *or* CLIENT **Operating system** OS/2

For DDE: HOTLINK NOTAB **Operating system** OS/2

UNBUF **Operating system** UNIX

ALQ=*n* CC=FORTRAN *or* PRINT *or* CR DEQ=*n* FAC=(DEL, GET, PUT, UPD)
KEY=*n* KEYVALUE ⟩ *or* ⟩= *or* ⟨ *or* ⟨= *value* MBC=*n* MBF=*n*
SHR=(DEL, GET, PUT, UPD, NONE) **Operating system** VMS

FORMAT

FORMAT *variable list format specification ... options*; ⁶⁶ Sets the format attribute of one or more variables.

Options

DEFAULT=*character format specification* The default format attribute for character variables that are created in the step.

DEFAULT=*numeric format specification* The default format attribute for numeric variables that are created in the step.

GOTO

GOTO *label*; ≡ Branches to the indicated statement label.

IF

IF *condition*; ≡ Subsetting: continues executing the current repetition of the observation loop only if the condition is true.

IF . . . THEN

IF *condition* THEN *action* ≡ Executes the action if the condition is true.

Example
```
IF X >= 0 THEN ROOT = SQRT(X);
ELSE ROOT = -SQRT(-X);
```

INFILE

INFILE *fileref or 'physical file name' options*; ≡ Sets the current input text file to the file indicated.

Options

Action taken when the INPUT statement reaches the end of a record before finding values for all its variables: MISSOVER It assigns missing values to the remaining variables. FLOWOVER It continues reading at column 1 of the next record. STOPOVER It creates an error condition, and the step stops running.

TRUNCOVER The same as MISSOVER, except that a short field at the end of the record is used where available. **Release** 6.07+

RECFM= Record format. Values vary by operating system. F Fixed length. V Variable length. U Undefined. D Data sensitive. N No format.

LRECL=*n* Logical record length: the number of characters in a record.

PAD Pads short records (shorter than the logical record length) with trailing blanks. This is the default for fixed-length records. NOPAD Does not pad with trailing blanks. This is the default for variable-length records.

LINESIZE *or* LS=*n* Line size: the maximum number of characters used in a record.

FIRSTOBS=*n* The first record to be read from the input file.

OBS=*n* The last record to be read from the input file.

N=*n* The number of lines available to the input pointer.

UNBUFFERED UNBUF Does not look ahead at the next record when reading a record.

EOF=*statement label* An INPUT statement branches to this statement label when it attempts to read past the end of the file.

END=*variable* A numeric variable that the INPUT statement sets to 1 when it reads the last record of the file. However, it does not do so if the UNBUFFERED option is used.

COLUMN *or* COL=*variable* A numeric variable that the INPUT statement sets to the column pointer location.

LINE=*variable* A numeric variable that the INPUT statement sets to the line pointer location.

LENGTH=*variable* A numeric variable that contains the length of the _INFILE_ string.

START=*variable* A numeric variable whose value indicates the first character to be used in the _INFILE_ string.

DELIMITERS *or* DLM='*chars*' *or variable* Delimiters used in list input. The default is DLM=' '.

DSD In list input, it treats each delimiter character separately and allows quoted strings with the ~ scanning control. **Release** 6.07+

EXPANDTABS Converts tab characters to blanks, using tab stops every 8 columns. NOEXPANDTABS Does not convert tabs. This is the default.

FILENAME=*variable* A character variable that shows the physical name of the file. **Release** 6.06+

FILEVAR=*variable* A character variable that can be used to change the physical input file. Changing the value of the variable causes the INFILE statement to close the input file and open the file whose physical name is the value of the variable. **Release** 6.06+

SHAREBUFFERS SHAREBUFS Uses the same buffer for input and output when the same fileref is used in an INFILE and a FILE statement in the same step.

BLKSIZE=*n* BLK=*n*

CCHHR=*variable* CLOSE=*position* DCB=*fileref* DEVTYPE=*variable*
DSCB=*variable* JFCB=*variable* UCBNAME=*variable*
VOL=*variable* **Operating system** MVS

For named pipes: BLOCK *or* NOBLOCK BYTE *or* MESSAGE EOFCONNECT
RETRY=*time* SERVER *or* CLIENT **Operating system** OS/2

For DDE: HOTLINK NOTAB **Operating system** OS/2

CC=FORTRAN *or* PRINT *or* CR FAC=(DEL, GET, PUT, UPD) KEY=*n*
KEYVALUE > *or* >= *or* < *or* <= *value* MBC=*n* MBF=*n*
SHR=(DEL, GET, PUT, UPD, NONE) **Operating system** VMS

INFORMAT

INFORMAT *variable list informat specification* ... *options*; **"** Sets the informat attribute of one or more variables.

Options

DEFAULT=*character informat specification* The default informat attribute for character variables that are created in the step.

DEFAULT=*numeric informat specification* The default informat attribute for numeric variables that are created in the step.

INPUT

INPUT *terms*; **≡** Reads from the current input text file. The terms can be one or more of the following:

@*n* @(*numeric expression*) @*numeric variable* Moves the column pointer to the indicated column.

@'*constant*' @(*character expression*) @*character variable* Moves the column pointer after the character indicated value.

+*n* +(*numeric expression*) +*numeric variable* Advances the column pointer the indicated number of columns.

/ Moves the line pointer to the next record, and changes the column pointer to 1.

#*n* #(*numeric expression*) #*numeric variable* Moves the line pointer to the indicated line and changes the column pointer to 1.

@ At the end of the INPUT statement, it holds the current input line(s). The input lines are released at the bottom of the observation loop.
@@ At the end of the INPUT statement, it holds the current input line(s). The input lines can be carried over to the next repetition of the observation loop.

(*variable list*) (*informat list*) Applies informats and pointer control terms to a list of variables.

variable term Reads a value for a variable. A variable term consists of a variable name or array element that is optionally followed by one or more of the following:

= Indicates *named input*. The variable name appears in the input record, followed by an equals sign and the variable value. Other variables can also appear in the input record.

$ Indicates a character variable.

: Scans. & Scans, and allows single embedded blanks. Scanning extracts a word and removes leading and trailing blanks.

~ Scans, and allows quoted strings if the DSD option is used in the INFILE statement. The quote marks are included as part of the value of a quoted string. **Release** 6.07+

? Suppresses data error messages.   ?? Ignores data errors.

informat specification Shows how to interpret the input data.
n n-n Reads from the indicated column or columns in the input line, using the standard informat. Otherwise, the variable is read using list input, using the variable's informat attribute or the standard informat.

Examples
List input:

```
LENGTH NAME $ 18 STATE $ 2;
INPUT NAME & AGE STATE;
```

Reading a fixed-field record:

```
INPUT @1 A 7. @8 B 7. @15 C $CHAR4. @20 D $CHAR1.;
```

KEEP

KEEP *variable list*;   "   Equivalent to the KEEP= dataset option for all output SAS datasets in the step. If the KEEP= or DROP= dataset option is also used on an output SAS dataset, the KEEP statement is applied first.

LABEL

LABEL *variable*='text' ... ...;   "   Sets the label attribute of one or more variables.

LEAVE

LEAVE;   ≡   Branches to the first statement after the (innermost) block. Use only in a DO loop, DO block, or SELECT block. **Release** 6.07+

LENGTH

LENGTH *variable list n or $ n ... option*;   "   Declares the length in bytes and the data type of variables. Use $ for character variables.

Option
DEFAULT=*n* Sets the default length in bytes of numeric variables. The default is DEFAULT=8.

LINK

LINK *label*;   ≡   Branches to the indicated statement label, then returns when a RETURN statement is executed.

Example
```
DATA ...;
  ...
  IF REPORTS < 1 THEN LINK MSG1;
  ...
  RETURN;
MSG1: FILE LOG;
  PUT 'No reports indicated for ' ID $CHAR. '. One report assumed.';
  REPORTS = 1;
  RETURN;
```

LIST

LIST;   ≡   Causes the input lines to be written to the log when the bottom of the observation loop is reached.

LOSTCARD

LOSTCARD;   ≡   Discards one record from the current input text file and restarts the current repetition of the observation loop.

MERGE

MERGE *SAS dataset SAS dataset ... option*;   ≡   One-to-one merge: Observations from two or more input SAS datasets are combined one at a time. The step stops when the end of all input SAS datasets is reached.

MERGE *SAS dataset SAS dataset ... option*; BY ...;   ≡   Match merge: Observations with matching values of BY variables from two or more input SAS datasets are combined. The step stops when the end of all input SAS datasets is reached.

Option

END=*variable*   A numeric variable whose value is set to 1 when the last observation is read.

MODIFY

MODIFY *SAS dataset options*;   ≡   Reads an observation from a SAS dataset open for editing. The SAS dataset must also be named in the DATA statement. You can use the REPLACE statement later to save changes to the observation, the REMOVE statement to delete the observation, or the DELETE statement to discard changes to the observation.

MODIFY *SAS dataset SAS dataset options*; BY ...;   ≡   Modifies values from the first SAS dataset with values from the second SAS dataset. The first SAS dataset must also be named in the DATA statement.

Options

END=*variable*   A numeric variable whose value is set to 1 when the last observation is read.

POINT=*variable*   A numeric variable whose value determines the observation number of the next observation to be read. To read an observation using direct access, assign a value to the POINT= variable, then execute the MODIFY statement with the POINT= option. The POINT= option cannot be used in combination with the BY statement.

NOBS=*variable*   A numeric variable whose value is the number of observations in the input SAS dataset(s) when the step begins.

KEY=*index* An existing index to be used in finding an observation in the SAS dataset. The MODIFY statement searches for an observation having values for the variables in the index that match the current values for those variables in the data step.
Release 6.07+

Null

;   ≡   No action.

OTHERWISE

OTHERWISE *action* ◆   In a SELECT block, it executes the action if none of the WHEN statements apply.

OUTPUT

OUTPUT; ≡   Writes an observation to all output SAS datasets in the data step, using the current values of data step variables.

OUTPUT *SAS dataset* ...; ≡   Writes an observation to the indicated SAS dataset(s). The SAS dataset(s) must have been named in the DATA statement. Dataset options cannot be used in the OUTPUT statement.

PUT

PUT *terms*; ≡   Writes to the current output text file. The terms can be one or more of the following:

@*n* @(*numeric expression*) @*numeric variable* Moves the column pointer to the indicated column.

@*'constant'* @(*character expression*) @*character variable* Moves the column pointer after the character indicated value.

+*n* +(*numeric expression*) +*numeric variable* Advances the column pointer the indicated number of columns.

/ Moves the line pointer to the next record and changes the column pointer to 1.

#*n* #(*numeric expression*) #*numeric variable* Moves the line pointer to the indicated line and changes the column pointer to 1.

@ @@ At the end of the PUT statement, it holds the current output line(s).

PAGE In a print file, it starts a new page.

BLANKPAGE In a print file, it starts a new page even if the current page is blank. **Release** 6.07+

variable term Writes a variable. A variable term consists of a variable name or array element optionally followed by one or more of the following:

= Indicates *named output*. The variable name is written followed by an equals sign and the variable value with leading and trailing blanks removed and a blank appended.

$ Indicates a character variable.

: Removes leading and trailing blanks and appends one blank.

format specification Shows how to format the value. *n   n-n* Writes to the indicated column or columns in the output line, using the variable's format attribute or the standard format. *n-n .n* Writes to the indicated columns in the output line, with the indicated number of decimal places. Otherwise, the variable is written using list output, using the variable's format attribute or the standard format, with leading and trailing blanks removed and a blank appended.

character constant Writes the character constant.

(*variable list*) (*format list*) Applies formatting and pointer-control terms to a list of variables.

ALL Equivalent to (_ALL_)(=).

INFILE Writes the _INFILE_ string, which is normally the last record read from the current input file.

Example

Writing a message:

```
PUT 'There were ' COUNT :COMMA11 'observations in ' PLACE +(-1) '.';
```

Writing a fixed-field record:

```
PUT @1 A 7. @8 B 7. @15 C $CHAR4. @20 D $CHAR1.;
```

Using a format list:

```
PUT (N1 X1 N2 X2 N3 X3 N4 X4 N5 X5) (8. +1 $CHAR2. +2);
```

REDIRECT

REDIRECT INPUT *or* OUTPUT *logical name=actual name* ... ; **❝** When running a compiled data step, it changes the name of an input or output SAS dataset. Used only after a DATA PGM= statement.

REMOVE

REMOVE; REMOVE *SAS dataset*...; Deletes an observation that was previously read with the MODIFY statement. If you use both the REMOVE and OUTPUT statements, execute the REMOVE statement before the OUTPUT statement. **Release** 6.07+

Example

This step removes some observations from the SAS dataset NEW. Notice that the REMOVE statement removes an observation, while the DELETE statement leaves the observation unchanged.

```
DATA NEW;
  MODIFY NEW;
  IF NAME IN (' ', 'X') THEN REMOVE;
  ELSE DELETE;
RUN;
```

RENAME

RENAME *variable=new name* ... ; ▪️ Equivalent to RENAME= dataset option for output SAS datasets. If the RENAME statement is used with the KEEP=, DROP=, or RENAME= dataset option on an output SAS dataset, the statement is applied before the dataset option.

REPLACE

REPLACE; REPLACE *SAS dataset* ... ; Updates an observation that was previously read with the MODIFY statement. If you use both the REPLACE and OUTPUT statements, execute the REPLACE statement before the OUTPUT statement. **Release** 6.07+

RETAIN

RETAIN *variable list value* ... ; ▪️ Keeps the variables from being automatically reset to missing and initializes them to the indicated value.

RETAIN; ▪️ Global RETAIN statement: keeps all variables from being automatically reset to missing.

RETURN

RETURN; ≡ After a LINK statement, it branches back to the statement following the LINK statement. After a HEADER= branch, it returns control to the PUT statement. Otherwise, it ends the current repetition of the observation loop; also it writes an observation to all output SAS datasets using the current values of the data step variables, unless an OUTPUT (or REPLACE or REMOVE) statement appears somewhere in the data step.

A RETURN statement is implied after the last statement in a data step.

RUN

RUN; } Marks the end of the step.

RUN CANCEL; } Cancels the step.

RUN PGM=*name*; } Compiles the step. **Release** 6.03–6.07

SELECT

SELECT(*expression*); WHEN(*expression*, ...) *action* ... OTHERWISE *action* END; ≡ Executes the action for the first WHEN expression that matches the SELECT expression, or executes the OTHERWISE action if no WHEN expression matches.

SELECT; WHEN(*condition*, ...) *action* ... OTHERWISE *action* END; ≡ Executes the action for the first true WHEN condition, or executes the OTHERWISE action if no WHEN condition is true.

Example
```
SELECT(NUMBER);
  WHEN(0) WORD = 'None';
  WHEN(1) WORD = 'One';
  OTHERWISE WORD = 'Some';
  END;
```

SET

SET *SAS dataset options*;   ≡   Reads an observation from an input SAS dataset.

SET;   ≡   The same as SET _LAST_;.

SET *SAS dataset SAS dataset ... options*;   ≡   Concatenate: reads an observation from one of the SAS datasets listed. The SAS datasets are combined end-to-end.

SET *SAS dataset SAS dataset ... options*; BY ...;   ≡   Interleave: reads an observation from one of the SAS datasets listed. The SAS datasets are combined in sorted order.

Options

END=*variable* A numeric variable whose value is set to 1 when the last observation is read.

POINT=*variable* A numeric variable whose value determines the observation number of the next observation to be read. To read an observation using direct access, assign a value to the POINT= variable, then execute the SET statement with the POINT= option. The POINT= option cannot be used in combination with the BY statement.

NOBS=*variable* A numeric variable whose value is the number of observation in the input SAS dataset(s).

KEY=*index* An existing index that is used to find an observation in the SAS dataset. The SET statement searches for an observation having values for the variables in the index that match the current values for those variables in the data step. **Release** 6.07+

STOP

STOP;   ≡   Stops execution of the data step.

Sum

numeric variable + expression;   ≡   Adds the expression (if not missing) to the numeric variable. The numeric variable is initialized to 0 and is not automatically reset to missing.

UPDATE

UPDATE *master SAS dataset transaction SAS dataset*; BY ...;   ≡   Modifies observations from the master SAS dataset with nonmissing values from observations in the transaction SAS dataset with the same values of BY variables. There should be only one observation in the master SAS dataset for each combination of values of BY variables. The default behavior of the observation loop is modified so that an implied OUTPUT occurs only after the last transaction observation is processed for a master observation. Thus, the UPDATE statement should not usually be used in combination with any other source of input data in a step.

Option

END=*variable* A numeric variable whose value is set to 1 when the last observation is read.

WHEN

WHEN(*condition or expression*) *action* ◆ In a SELECT block, it executes the action if the condition is true or the expression equals the SELECT expression.

WHERE

WHERE *condition* ; " Equivalent to the WHERE= dataset option for all input SAS datasets.

WHERE ALSO *condition* ; " Adds an additional condition to a previous WHERE statement.

WHERE UNDO; " Removes the effect of the most recent WHERE statement.

WHERE CLEAR; WHERE; " Removes the effect of all preceding WHERE statements.

WINDOW

WINDOW *name window options field . . . group . . .*; " Defines a window that can then be displayed by the DISPLAY statement.

Window options

COLOR=*color* The background color for the window.

ROWS=*n* COLUMNS=*n* IROW=*n* ICOLUMN=*n* Sets the window size and location.

MENU=*PMENU entry* The window displays the menu bar that is defined by the PMENU entry in PMENU mode.

KEYS=*KEYS entry* The function key definitions of the KEYS entry are used in the window.

Fields

A *field* can be a constant field, a protected variable field, or an unprotected variable field. A window must have at least one field or group.

pointer controls 'constant' field options A constant field: the constant value is displayed at the indicated location.

pointer controls variable optional format specification PROTECT=YES *field options* A protected variable field: the value of the variable is displayed at the indicated location. If the format specification is omitted, the variable's format attribute or the standard format is used.

pointer controls variable optional informat/format specification field options An unprotected variable field: the value of the variable is displayed at the indicated location and can be modified by the user. The format specification must also be a valid informat specification. If the format specification is omitted, the variable's informat and format attributes or the standard informat and format are used.

Pointer controls

#*n* #*numeric variable* #(*numeric expression*) Moves the line pointer to the line indicated.

/ Moves the line pointer to the next line.

If no line pointer control is used, a field is placed on the same line as the previous field, or on line 1.

@*n* @*numeric variable* @(*numeric expression*)   Moves the column pointer to the indicated column.

+*n* +*numeric variable* +(*numeric expression*)   Advances the column pointer by the indicated number of columns.

If no column pointer control is used, a field is placed immediately after the preceding field, or at the beginning of the line.

Field options

COLOR *or* C=*color*   The color of text displayed in the field.

ATTR *or* A=(*video attribute*, ...)   Video attributes of text displayed in the field. HIGHLIGHT Highlighting. REV_VIDEO Reverse video. BLINK Blinking. UNDERLINE Underlining.

PROTECT *or* P=YES A protected variable field. PROTECT *or* P=NO An unprotected variable field. This is the default.

PERSIST=YES The contents of a field remain displayed when the screen is redisplayed. PERSIST=NO The contents of the field disappear when the screen is redisplayed. This is the default.

REQUIRED=YES A user is not allowed to leave the field blank. Use this only for unprotected variable fields. REQUIRED=NO A user is allowed to leave the field blank. This is the default.

AUTOSKIP *or* AUTO=YES Moves the cursor to the next unprotected field in the window after the user types a character in the last position of the field. AUTOSKIP *or* AUTO=NO Does not automatically move the cursor. This is the default.

DISPLAY=YES Displays the field. This is the default. DISPLAY=NO Hides the field.

Groups

A window can have one or more *groups* that are displayed separately. A group is defined as:

GROUP=*name* field ...

A group must contain at least one field.

6

Proc step statements

The statements that can be used in a proc step depend on the proc being run. However, a common set of proc step statements can be used in most procs.

ATTRIB

ATTRIB *variable attributes* ...; Declares one or more attributes for a variable. Attributes can be one or more of the following:

LENGTH=*n* or LENGTH=$ *n* The length of the variable, in bytes. Use $ for a character variable.

INFORMAT=*informat specification*

FORMAT=*format specification*

LABEL='*label*' A descriptive phrase that can be up to 40 characters long.

BY

BY *variables options*; Indicates that the input SAS dataset(s) is (are) sorted or grouped by the indicated variables. Most procs process each BY group separately. The keyword DESCENDING can appear before a variable to indicate that the variable is sorted in descending order.

Options

NOTSORTED Indicates that the input data is grouped, but not necessarily sorted.

GROUPFORMAT Forms groups that are based on the formatted values of the variables.

Example

You can use either BY SIZE; or BY SIZE NOTSORTED; to have the input SAS dataset processed in groups formed by values of SIZE. If you use BY SIZE; an error occurs if the values of SIZE are not sorted in ascending order.

FORMAT

FORMAT *variable list format specification* ...; Sets the format attribute of one or more variables.

INFORMAT

INFORMAT *variable list informat specification* ...; Sets the informat attribute of one or more variables.

LABEL

LABEL *variable*='*text*' ... ... ;   Sets the label attribute of one or more variables.

PROC

PROC *proc options*;   The first statement in a proc step. Identifies the proc being run and supplies options for the proc.

QUIT

QUIT;   Marks the end of the step.

RUN

RUN;   In most procs, this statement marks the end of the step. In run-group procs, it marks the end of a run group.

RUN CANCEL;   Cancels the step or, in a run-group proc, the run group.

WHERE

WHERE *condition*;   Equivalent to the WHERE= dataset option for all input SAS datasets.

WHERE ALSO *condition*;   Adds an additional condition to a previous WHERE statement.

WHERE UNDO;   Removes the effect of the most recent WHERE statement.

WHERE CLEAR;   WHERE;   Removes the effect of all preceding WHERE statements.

7

Expressions

An *expression* represents a single value that is used in a program. A SAS expression can be a constant, variable, or array element, or it can combine constants and variables with function calls and operators. Constants are used at various places in SAS programs. Other expressions are used mainly in the data step.

Data types

Each SAS expression belongs to one of two *data types*. The numeric data type holds numeric data in a double-precision format. The character data type can hold any kind of data and can have a length of up to 200 bytes.

Variables

Variables can be referred to by their names or as array elements. The name of a variable cannot be the same as the name of an array in the same step. Variables are used in expressions, as arguments to some routines, and in some statement options. Within a data step, a variable can have only one data type. The data type is determined by the first appearance of the variable in the step.

In addition to variables that are named in the data step and those that are created as array elements, a data step can contain the automatic variables listed here.

CMD

A value entered by the user in the command line of a data step window that is not recognized as a display manager command.

ERROR

Boolean: 1 if an error has been detected in the current repetition of the observation loop, or 0 otherwise.

_I_

The index variable that is used for implicitly subscripted arrays when no index variable is named in the ARRAY statement.

IORC

A system return code from an I/O action on an observation in a SAS dataset. This variable is set by the MODIFY statement and the SET statement with the KEY= option. **Release** 6.07+

MSG

A message to be displayed in a data step window.

_N_

Counts the repetitions of the observation loop, starting with 1.

FIRST.*variable*

Boolean for each BY variable: 1 if the current observation is the first one in the group that is formed by the BY variable and all earlier BY variables, 0 otherwise.

LAST.*variable*

Boolean for each BY variable: 1 if the current observation is the last one in the group that is formed by the BY variable and all earlier BY variables, 0 otherwise.

Constants

Constants are data values that appear in a program.

Decimal

Decimal constants represent the ordinary way of writing numbers, except that commas are not used. A minus sign can be used to indicate a negative number.

```
23
-.03125
50000
```

Missing

A numeric missing value indicates the absence of a number in a place where a numeric value is expected. A standard missing value is represented by a period. A special missing value is represented by a period followed by a letter or underscore.

Scientific

Scientific notation follows a decimal constant with an E and then an integer that indicates a power of 10.

```
6.02E23
```

Hexadecimal

Hexadecimal notation is a way of writing integers in base 16, with the letters A–F used as the digits 10–15. The constant value is followed by an X and cannot begin with a letter.

```
0C053X
```

SAS date

A SAS date is a number that represents the number of days elapsed since the beginning of 1960. A SAS date constant is an integer value represented in date form, with the day of month, 3-letter month abbreviation, and year, quoted and followed by the letter D.

'31DEC1999'D

SAS time

A SAS time is the number of seconds since midnight. A SAS time constant shows hours, minutes, and optionally seconds, separated by colons, quoted, and followed by the letter T.

'15:38:00.00'T

SAS datetime

A SAS datetime is the number of seconds since the beginning of 1960. A SAS datetime constant combines the notation of a SAS date constant and a SAS time constant. It is quoted and followed by the letters DT.

'01JAN1960 00:00:00'DT

Character literal

A character literal is an ordinary character constant. It is a quoted string. The characters in the quoted string are the actual constant value.

'constant'

However, to represent a quote mark in the character constant, use two quote marks.

'Isn"t'

Character hexadecimal

Character hexadecimal notation uses two hexadecimal digits to represent each byte of data. A character hexadecimal constant must contain an even number of digits, but not more than 200 in all. It is quoted and followed by the letter X.

'4241'X

Operators

An *operator* acts on one or two expressions to form a new expression. Most operators form values of a particular data type, indicated by N or $ in the entries below. Each SAS operator uses either one operand or two, as indicated.

The comparison operators produce numeric values, either a 1 (indicating true) or a 0 (indicating false). The logical operators treat nonzero numbers as true, and 0 and missing values as false.

When missing values are used with the comparison and MAX and MIN operators, they compare less than numbers.

*

$a*b$ **N** Multiplication: a times b.

**

$a**b$ **N** Exponentiation: a raised to the power of b.

+

$+a$ **N** Identity; a.
$a + b$ **N** Addition: a plus b.

−

$-a$ **N** Negation: the negative of a.
$a - b$ **N** Subtraction: a minus b.

/

a/b **N** Division: a divided by b.

AND

a AND b **N** And: 1 if a and b are both true, 0 otherwise.
Also written as &

Comparison

$a < b$ Is less than. **Also written as** LT
$a <= b$ Is less than or equal to. **Also written as** LE
$a = b$ Equals. **Also written as** EQ
$a >= b$ Is greater than or equal to. **Also written as** GE
$a > b$ Is greater than. **Also written as** GT
a NE b Does not equal. **Also written as** ^=, ¬=, ~=, NOT=, etc.
a IN ($constant, ...$) Is in.
a NOTIN ($constant, ...$) Is not in. **Also written as** ^IN, ¬IN
N Comparison: 1 if the comparison is true, 0 otherwise. With character operands of unequal lengths, the shorter operand is treated as padded with blanks to the length of the longer operand.

$a <: b$ **Also written as** LT:
$a <=: b$ **Also written as** LE:
$a =: b$ **Also written as** EQ:
$a >=: b$ **Also written as** GE:
$a >: b$ **Also written as** GT:
a NE: b **Also written as** ^=:, ¬=:, ~=:, NOT=:, etc.
a IN: ($constant, ...$)
a NOTIN: ($constant, ...$) **Also written as** ^IN:, ¬IN:
N Character comparison with truncation: 1 if the comparison, with the longer operand treated as being truncated to the length of the shorter operand, is true, 0 otherwise.

*a = 'bit mask '*B   **Also written as** EQ
N   Bit testing. The bit mask is a string of 0s, 1s, and periods. Spaces can also be included for clarity. Each character in the bit mask represents a bit. The bit mask is compared against the operand *a* bit by bit. If the expression is numeric, it is converted to a 32-bit integer and right-aligned against the bit mask. If the expression is character, it is left-aligned. The comparison is true if all the 0s and 1s in the bit mask match the corresponding bits in the expression.

MAX

a MAX *b*   **$N**   Maximum; the greater of the values *a* and *b*.
Also written as <>

MIN

a MIN *b*   **$N**   Minimum; the lesser of the values *a* and *b*.
Also written as ><

NOT

NOT *a*   **N**   Logical not: 1 if *a* is false, 0 otherwise.
Also written as ^, ¬, ~

OR

a OR *b*   **N**   Or: 1 if either *a* or *b* is true, 0 if both *a* and *b* are false.
Also written as |

||

a || *b*   **$**   Concatenation; *a* with *b* added to the end.

Compound expressions

In an expression with more than one operator, parentheses can be used to control the order in which the operators are applied:

A + (B*C)

If parentheses are not used to isolate each operator, the sequence of operators is determined by the priority of each operator. When two or more operators have the same priority, they are executed in order, either left to right or right to left. Operator priorities are shown in this table:

Operators	Priority	Order
Prefix (NOT, +, -), MIN, MAX, **	1 (first)	right to left
*, /	2	left to right
+, - (addition, subtraction)	3	left to right
||	4	left to right
Comparison	5	left to right
AND	6	left to right
OR	7 (last)	left to right

Examples

A OR B AND C is evaluated as A OR (B AND C), because AND has a higher priority than OR.

A – B – C is evaluated as (A – B) – C, because the subtraction operator is evaluated from left to right.

WHERE operators

WHERE expressions, also called WHERE clauses, are conditions used in the WHERE= dataset option and elsewhere to subset input SAS datasets. They can use constants, variables in the SAS dataset, SAS function calls, and operators (prior to release 6.07, WHERE expressions cannot use function calls).

The MAX operator can be used, but must be written MAX, not <>. These additional Boolean operators can be used in WHERE clauses:

a BETWEEN *b* AND *c*   **N**   Boolean: 1 if *a* is the range between *b* and *c*, 0 otherwise.

a NOT BETWEEN *b* and *c*   **N**   Boolean: 1 if *a* is outside the range between *b* and *c*, 1 if it is in the range

a CONTAINS *b*   *a* ? *b*   **N**   Boolean: 1 if *b* is a substring of *a*, 0 otherwise. **Release** 6.06+

a NOT CONTAINS *b*   *a* NOT ? *b*   **N**   Boolean: 1 if *b* is not a substring of *a*, 0 if it is. **Release** 6.06+

a IS NULL   *a* IS MISSING   **N**   Boolean: 1 if *a* is a missing (or blank) value, 0 otherwise.

a IS NOT NULL   *a* IS NOT MISSING   *a* NOT IS NULL   *a* NOT IS MISSING   *a* IS ^ NULL   *etc.*   **N**   Boolean: 1 if *a* is a nonmissing (or nonblank) value, 0 otherwise.

a LIKE *b*   **N**   Character comparison with wild-card characters; similar to the = operator, but in in the second operand, _ matches any character in the first operand, and ? matches any sequence of characters.   **Release** 6.06+

a NOT LIKE *b*   **N**   Similar to the NE operator, but with the wild-card characters _ and ?. **Release** 6.06+

a =* *b*   *a* EQ* *b*   **N**   Sounds-like: tests whether two character operands sound the same, according to the Soundex algorithm. **Release** 6.06+

Character sets

A computer's *character set*, or *collating sequence*, determines what characters the computer can display and the comparison order of character data.

ASCII

Most computers use the ASCII character set with additional characters.

	0	1	2	3	4	5	6	7	8	9	A	B	C	D	E	F
0																
1																
2	space	!	"	#	$	%	&	'	(	)	*	+	,	–	.	/
3	0	1	2	3	4	5	6	7	8	9	:	;	<	=	>	?
4	@	A	B	C	D	E	F	G	H	I	J	K	L	M	N	O
5	P	Q	R	S	T	U	V	W	X	Y	Z	[	\	]	^	_
6	`	a	b	c	d	e	f	g	h	i	j	k	l	m	n	o
7	p	q	r	s	t	u	v	w	x	y	z	{	|	}	~	
8																
9																
A																
B																
C																
D																
E																
F																

EBCDIC

The EBCDIC character set is used by IBM mainframes.

	0	1	2	3	4	5	6	7	8	9	A	B	C	D	E	F
0																
1																
2																
3																
4	blank										¢	.	<	(	+	|
5	&										!	$	*	)	;	¬
6	–	/									|	,	%	_	>	?
7										`	:	#	@	'	=	"
8		a	b	c	d	e	f	g	h	i						
9		j	k	l	m	n	o	p	q	r						
A		~	s	t	u	v	w	x	y	z						
B																
C	{	A	B	C	D	E	F	G	H	I						
D	}	J	K	L	M	N	O	P	Q	R						
E	\		S	T	U	V	W	X	Y	Z						
F	0	1	2	3	4	5	6	7	8	9						

Arrays

An *array* is a named list of variables in a data step. It is defined in the ARRAY statement. The name of an array should not be the same as the name of a variable in the same data step or the name of a SAS function.

After an array is defined, a variable in the array can be used by referring to the array. An array reference is formed by following the array name with the subscript value in braces:

array{subscript}

The subscript can be any numeric expression, but you should make sure it resolves to an integer value within the array's subscript range. You can use parentheses in places of braces.

For a multidimensional array, two or more subscripts are separated by commas:

array{subscript, subscript}

Array names can be used as abbreviated variable lists in some statements. A previously defined array name can be listed in a RETAIN statement to provide initial values for the array elements. In a PUT statement or INPUT statement, you can list all the elements of an array by using $\star$ in place of an array subscript:

PUT *array{$\star$}*;

Lengths of character expressions

The length of a character expression results from the variable and constant values and the operators and functions that make up the expression. If a character expression is assigned to a character variable with a different length, the expression is altered to fit the length of the variable. If the expression is shorter than the variable, trailing blanks are added, a process called *blank padding*. If the expression is longer than the variable, characters are omitted from the end of the expression. That process is called *truncation*.

Example
```
LENGTH A $ 4;
A = 'INFORMATION';
PUT A=;
```
_____

A=INFO

Automatic type conversion

If a numeric expression is assigned to a character variable or used in another place where a character expression is expected, a character value is created by applying the BEST format to the numeric value. The resulting character value often contains leading blanks.

Similarly, character expressions are automatically converted to numeric values as needed using the standard numeric informat.

Missing values

Numeric *missing values* are numeric values that represent the absence of a number. Blank character values are also missing values. Missing values can appear in input text data or as constant values in the program. They are also generated in many situations when a program is run. By default, ordinary variables in a data step are initialized to missing, and many of them are reset to missing at the beginning of each repetition of the observation loop. Missing values are also created by the SET statement when SAS datasets contain different variables and by the MERGE statement when not all observations match.

Numeric missing values result when invalid values are read from input files or are used as arguments to functions, when missing values are used as operands for arithmetic operators, and when an automatic type conversion of a character value to a numeric value is unsuccessful. In comparisons, numbers are considered to be greater than missing values.

8

Dataset options

At most places where a SAS dataset is used in a SAS program, *dataset options* can be used to modify the way the SAS dataset is read or written. Dataset options appear in parentheses after the SAS dataset name:

> *SAS dataset (dataset option   dataset option   ...)*

Dataset options might be valid when a SAS dataset is created (**C**), modified (**M**), or read (**R**), as indicated in the entries below. Some dataset options have the same name and purpose as system options. Use the dataset option to override the system option for a specific SAS dataset.

ALTER=

password Assigns a password for alter-protection or accesses an alter-protected SAS file. **Release** 6.07+

BUFNO=

C

n Number of buffers to use for each SAS dataset.

BUFSIZE=

C

n or nK or nM or nG Number of bytes in internal I/O buffer.

CNTLLEV=

MR

MEM Member control level: the entire SAS dataset is locked.
REC Record control level: the SAS dataset is locked one observation at a time.

COMPRESS=

C

YES Observations in the SAS dataset are stored in a compressed form.
NO Observations are not compressed.

DROP=

CR

variables The list of variables to be excluded.

FILECLOSE=

The position of a tape volume when a SAS dataset is closed:
REREAD At the beginning of the file. LEAVE At the end of the file.
REWIND FREE At the beginning of the volume. DISP As set by operating system. Overrides the TAPECLOSE= system option. Values vary by operating system.

FIRSTOBS=

R

n The first observation to be processed from input file. Use this option to skip observations at the beginning of a SAS dataset.

IN=

R

variable Creates a logical variable that shows whether an observation comes from the specified SAS dataset. It is used only in SET, MERGE, MODIFY, and UPDATE statements.

INDEX=

C

(*index definition . . . options*)   Defines indexes for a SAS dataset.

Index definitions

variable A *simple index*, which uses only one variable. The variable name is also used as the index name.

index=(*variable variable . . .*)   A *composite index*, which uses two or more variables. The index name cannot be the same as the name of a variable.

Options

NOMISS Excludes observations that have missing values for any key variable in the index.

UNIQUE Prevents creation of additional observations with the same key values as any existing observation.
Release 6.07+

KEEP=

CR

variables Variables to be read from or written to the SAS dataset.

LABEL=

CR

'*description*' Descriptive label for the SAS dataset.

OBS=

R

n or MAX Processing from an input file stops at the observation number specified.

PW=

password Assigns a password to protect a SAS file from being read, written, and altered; or accesses a password-protected SAS file. **Release** 6.07+

READ=

password Assigns a password for read-protection or accesses a read-protected SAS file. **Release** 6.07+

RENAME=

CR

(*variable=new name* ...) Changes variable names. If you use the KEEP= dataset option for the same SAS dataset, use the old variable names in the KEEP= option.

REPLACE=

C

When the SAS dataset being created has the same name as an existing SAS dataset: YES Replaces the existing SAS dataset with the new SAS dataset. NO Creates an error condition.

REUSE=

C

YES Allows the space of deleted observations to be reused in a compressed SAS dataset. NO Does not allow the space of deleted observations to be reused in a compressed SAS dataset.

SORTEDBY=

sort order / optional collating sequence Indicates how observations in the SAS dataset are currently sorted.

NULL Indicates that observations are not necessarily in sorted order.

Release 6.07+

TYPE=

SAS dataset type A code used by some SAS procs to identify special types of SAS datasets.

WHERE=

R

(*condition*) Selects observations to be processed.

WRITE=

password Assigns a password for write-protection or accesses a write-protected SAS file. **Release** 6.07+

9

System options

System options allow you to control the way things work in a SAS session.

Most system options can be changed at any time during the SAS session. Some, marked **Init.** in the entries that follow, are initialization options that can be set only at the beginning of the SAS session, either in the command line or configuration file.

During a session, options are changed in the OPTIONS statement. In the OPTIONS statement, keyword options appear simply as the option name to turn the option on, or the option name prefixed by NO to turn the option off. For keyword-value options, the option name is followed by an equals sign (=) and an appropriate value for the option.

Many options can also be changed in the OPTIONS window.

ALTLOG=

'physical file name' or device **Init.** A copy of the log is directed to this file.

ALTPRINT=

'physical file name' or device **Init.** A copy of the standard print file is directed to this file.

AUTOEXEC=

'physical file name' **Init.** SAS statements in this file are executed at the beginning of the session.
Alias AE

BATCH

Init. ON The batch set of option defaults is used.
OFF The interactive set of option defaults is used if the session is in the foreground. **Operating system** Multiuser

BUFNO=

n The number of buffers to use for each SAS dataset.

BUFSIZE=

n The number of bytes in the internal I/O buffer.

BYERR

When an attempt is made to sort a SAS dataset with no variables: ON An error is generated. OFF No action is taken. **Release** 6.07+

BYLINE

ON Procs print BY lines that identify each BY group. OFF Procs do not print BY lines. Each BY group starts on a separate page.
Release 6.07+

CAPS

ON Lowercase letters in the SAS program are treated as capital letters.
OFF Lowercase letters are treated as lowercase letters.

CARDIMAGE

ON Source and data lines are processed as 80-character lines. Tokens can be split between lines. OFF The last nonblank character is treated as the end of the line of input and is a token boundary.

CATCACHE=

n The specified number of SAS catalogs is kept open.

CENTER

ON Title lines, footnote lines, and most print output from procs are centered horizontally on the page.
OFF Print output is left-aligned on the page.

Alias CENTRE

CHARCODE

ON Special character combinations can be used to substitute for characters that are not on the keyboard:

?: for '	?, for \	?(for {	?) for }	?= for ^ or ¬
?- for _	?/ for |	?< for [	?> for]	

OFF Substitute character combinations are not recognized.

CLEANUP

ON Automatically frees memory, as needed, by removing unnecessary resources. OFF Does not free memory automatically.

CMDMAC

ON The macro processor recognizes command-style macro invocations for command-style macros. OFF The macro processor does not recognize command-style macro invocations. **Release** 6.07+

COMAMID=

communications access method A communications access method that is used by SAS/CONNECT and SAS/SHARE software.

COMPRESS=

YES *or* NO Equivalent to the dataset option.

CONFIG=

'physical file name' **Init.** The file that contains system options that are set at the start of the session. Valid only on the command line.

CPUID

Init. ON   At the beginning of the SAS session, a note identifying the hardware is written in the log.   **Release** 6.07+

DATE

ON   The date and time are printed in the log and the title lines of any print file.   OFF   The date and time are not printed in title lines.

DBCS

ON   The SAS System recognizes double-byte character sets.
OFF   Only single-byte character sets can be used.

DBCSLANG=

character set   The double-byte character set to be used.

DBCSTYPE=

coding method   The coding method that is used for double-byte character sets.

DETAILS

ON   SAS data library directory listings contain additional information, such as dataset labels.   OFF   SAS data library directory listings contain standard information.   **Release** 6.07+

DEVICE=

driver   The terminal device driver that is used by SAS/GRAPH software.
Alias DEV

DKRICOND=

When a DROP=, KEEP=, or RENAME= dataset option for an input SAS dataset uses a variable name incorrectly:
ERROR   An error condition is generated.
WARN   WARNING   A warning message is generated.
NOWARN   NOWARNING   The incorrect reference is ignored.
Release 6.07+

DKROCOND

When a DROP=, KEEP=, or RENAME= dataset option for an output SAS dataset or a DROP, KEEP, or RENAME statement uses a variable name incorrectly:
ERROR   An error condition is generated.
WARN   WARNING   A warning message is generated.
NOWARN   NOWARNING   The incorrect reference is ignored.
Release 6.07+

DMR

Init. ON   Allows SAS/CONNECT software to start a remote session.
OFF   Prevents a remote session.

DMS

Init. ON Display manager windows are displayed throughout the session.
OFF Display manager is not active in the session.

DSNFERR

When a specified input SAS dataset is not found: ON An error message is generated. OFF A _NULL_ input SAS dataset, with no variables, is used.

ECHOAUTO

Init. ON Statements from the AUTOEXEC file are written to the log.
OFF Statements from the AUTOEXEC file are not written to the log.

ENGINE=

engine The default engine for SAS data libraries.

ERRORABEND

ON The SAS System abends under most error conditions.
OFF Most error conditions do not cause an abend.

Alias ERRABEND

ERRORS=

n For data errors, the maximum number of observations for which complete error messages are printed.

FIRSTOBS=

n The first record or observation to be processed from an input file.

FMTERR

When the format of a variable's format attribute cannot be found: ON An error message is generated. OFF The default format is used.

FMTSEARCH=

(*libref or catalog* ...) When an informat or format is used, format catalogs are searched in the order listed. If a one-level name is stated, the catalog FORMATS in that library is searched. The default catalogs WORK.FORMATS and LIBRARY.FORMATS are searched first and second unless you list them in a different position in the search order. **Release 6.07+**

FORMCHAR=

'*chars*' Formatting characters that are used in the print output of some procs. These characters are used mainly for printing tables.

Default '|----|+|---+=|-/\<>*'

FORMDLIM=

'*char*' A character that replaces page breaks in print output.

' ' Actual page breaks are used in print output. This is the default.

Alias FRMDLIM

FORMS=

form The default form that is used for customizing printed output from windows.

Alias FRMS

FSDEVICE=

driver The interactive windowing device driver for the terminal being used.

FULLSTATS

Equivalent to the FULLSTIMER system option. **Operating system** MVS

FULLSTIMER

ON Statistics that are written in the log for each step are written in an expanded format with more detail.

GWINDOW

ON Graphics output can be displayed in the GRAPH window of display manager. OFF There is no GRAPH window, and graphics output is displayed outside of display manager.

IMPLMAC

ON The macro processor recognizes statement-style macro invocations for statement-style macros. OFF The macro processor does not recognize statement-style macro invocations.

INITSTMT=

'statement(s)' **Init.** These statements are executed at the beginning of the SAS session after statements from the AUTOEXEC file and before statements from the SYSIN file.

Alias IS

INVALIDDATA=

char A character that represents the missing value produced by informats for invalid numeric data. **Default** INVALIDDATA='.'

LABEL

ON Procs can print variable labels.
OFF Variable labels are not available to procs.

LINESIZE=

n The length of the line that is used in print files.
Alias LS

LOG=

'physical file name' or device **Init.** The file to which the log is written.
Mode Other than display manager

MACRO

ON The macro processor is active; macrolanguage objects can be used.

OFF The macro processor is inactive; the use of macrolanguage objects results in an error condition.

MAPS=

libref or 'physical file name' The SAS data library that contains the SAS/GRAPH map datasets. **Release** 6.07+

MAUTOSOURCE

ON Macros in autocall libraries can be used.
OFF Macros in autocall libraries cannot be used.

MEMRPT

ON The SAS System records memory statistics from the operating system for each step. OFF The SAS System does not record memory statistics for each step. **Operating system** MVS

MERROR

ON The macro processor writes a warning message if a macro reference (a percent sign followed by a name) cannot be matched to a macro keyword or macro name. OFF The macro processor ignores macro references that cannot be matched to macro keywords or macro names.

MISSING=

char The character that is printed for missing values of numeric variables. **Default** MISSING='.'

MLOGIC

ON Macro control flow is described in the log.
OFF Macro control flow is not described in the log.

MPRINT

ON SAS statements generated by macros are written in the log.
OFF SAS statements generated by macros are not written in the log.

MRECALL

ON The macro processor searches the autocall libraries for a macro, even if it was not found in an earlier search. OFF If a macro was not previously found, the search is not repeated.

MSGCASE

Init. ON SAS System messages are printed and displayed in all uppercase letters. OFF SAS System messages are printed and displayed in upper- and lowercase letters. **Release** 6.07+

MSGLEVEL=

I Extra log notes and warnings are generated.
N The standard notes and warnings are generated. **Release** 6.07+

MSTORED

ON The macro catalog in the library specified by the SASMSTORE= option is used to store macros compiled with the STORE option and is searched for called macros that are not found in the WORK.SASMACR catalog.

OFF   The STORE option is ignored and only the WORK.SASMACR catalog is searched for called macros. **Release 6.07+**

MSYMTABMAX=

n or nK or nM or nG or MAX   The maximum amount of memory used by all macrovariables. **Release 6.07+**

MVARSIZE=

n or nK or nM or nG or MAX   The maximum size of a macrovariable that is kept in memory. **Release 6.07+**

NEWS=

'physical file name' **Init.**   Messages from this file, typically bulletins for SAS users in multi-user installations, are written to the SAS log.

NOTES

ON   Notes are written to the log.
OFF   Notes are not written to the log.
Alias LNOTES

NUMBER

ON   The page number appears on the first title line of each page of print output. OFF   The page number does not appear in title lines.

OBS=

n or MAX   The last observation or record read from an input file. Subsequent observations or records are ignored.

OPLIST

Init. ON   The settings of SAS system options at the start of the SAS session are written to the log.

OVP

ON   Print files can contain overprinting.
OFF   Overprinting is not allowed.

PAGENO=

n   The page number for the next page of print output.
Alias PAGNO

PAGESIZE=

n   The number of lines per page in print output.
Alias PS

PARM=

'string'   The parameter string passed to an external program.

PARMCARDS=

fileref The file that is opened by a PARMCARDS statement.

PRINT=

'physical file name' or device **Init.** The standard print file.
Mode Other than display manager

PROBSIG=

0, 1, *or* 2 The minimum number of significant digits that are printed for
p-values by certain statistical procs.

PROC

ON Programs other than SAS System procs — SAS/TOOLKIT procs, for
example — can be invoked in the PROC statement.
OFF Only SAS System procs can be invoked in the PROC statement.
Release 6.07+

PROCLEAVE=

n The amount of memory that is set aside to allow for proc termination
under certain error conditions.

REMOTE=

session ID **Init.** The session ID for a remote session.

REPLACE

Equivalent to the dataset option. Does not apply to scratch SAS data
libraries.

REUSE=

YES *or* NO Equivalent to the dataset option.

S=

n The maximum length of lines in a program file.

S2=

n The maximum length of lines in %INCLUDE files. **Default** The value of
the S= option

SASAUTOS=

('*storage location*', ...) The autocall library or libraries.

SASFRSCR=

fileref **SCL only, Read-only** The fileref generated by the SAS System for the
script files that are specified in the SASSCRIPT= system option. **Release**
6.07+

SASHELP=

'physical file name' **Init.** The SAS data library that contains SAS System
help files.

SASMSG=

'*physical file name*' **Init.** The SAS data library that contains SAS System messages.

SASMSTORE=

libref The SAS data library that contains the SASMACR catalog of compiled macros used in the session. **Release** 6.07+

SASSCRIPT=

('*storage location*' ...) The aggregate storage location(s) for SAS/CONNECT scripts. **Release** 6.07+

SASUSER=

'*physical file name*' **Init.** The SASUSER library, which contains the user profile catalog.

SEQ=

n $1 \le n \le 8$ The length of the numeric portion of the sequence-number field in SAS source lines.

SERROR

ON The macro processor writes a warning message if a macrovariable reference (an ampersand followed by a name) cannot be matched to a macrovariable. OFF The macro processor ignores macrovariable references that cannot be matched to macrovariables.

SETINIT

Init. ON SAS System site license information can be altered.
OFF SAS System site license information cannot be altered.

SITEINFO=

'*physical file name*' **Init.** The file that contains site-specific information about the SAS System.

SKIP=

n $0 \le n \le 20$ The number of lines that are skipped at the top of each page in a print file before the title lines. **Release** 6.07+

SORTPGM=

program The name of the sorting utility program that is used by the SAS System.

SORTSEQ=

collating sequence The default collating sequence that is used when sorting SAS datasets. **Release** 6.07+

SORTSIZE=

n or *n*K or *n*M or MAX The maximum amount of memory available to the sort routine when sorting SAS datasets.
Release 6.07+

Alias SSIZE

SOURCE

ON SAS source statements are written to the log.
OFF Source statements are not written to the log.

SOURCE2

ON Secondary source statements (from files included by %INCLUDE
statements) are written to the log.
OFF Secondary source statements are not written to the log.

Alias SRC2

SPOOL

ON SAS statements are written to a utility dataset in the WORK library
for later use, for example by %INCLUDE or %LIST statements. OFF SAS
statements are discarded after they are executed.

STATS

ON Performance statistics are written in the log for each step, if available.
OFF Performance statistics are not written in the log for each step.
Operating system MVS

STAX

ON Attention interrupts are handled by the operating system.
OFF The session ends when the user presses the attention key.
Operating system MVS

STIMER

ON The SAS System records performance statistics from the operating
system for each step. OFF The SAS System does not record performance
statistics for each step.

SYMBOLGEN

ON The macro processor displays the result of resolving macro references.
OFF The result of resolving macro references is not displayed.

Alias SGEN

SYSIN=

'*physical file name*' **Init.** The specified SAS program file is executed after
the AUTOEXEC file and INITSTMT= statements.

SYSLEAVE=

n The amount of memory that is set aside to allow for SAS System
termination under certain error conditions.

SYSPARM=

'*string*' The SYSPARM() function call and the &SYSPARM macrovariable
reference can be used to refer to this character string.

TAPECLOSE=

The position of a tape volume when a SAS data library is closed:
REREAD At the beginning of the file. LEAVE At the end of the file.
REWIND At the beginning of the volume. DISP As set by operating
system. Values vary by operating system.

TERMINAL

Init. ON A terminal is connected to the SAS session.
OFF No terminal is connected.
Default ON in interactive mode, OFF in batch mode.

TRANTAB=

(*local-to-transport translation table name,*
transport-to-local translation table name,
lowercase-to-uppercase translation table name,
uppercase-to-lowercase translation table name,
character classification translation table name,
scanner translation table name,
delta characters translation table name,
scanner character classification translation table name) Translation tables
that are used by the SAS System. **Release** 6.07+

USER=

'*physical file name*' *or libref* One-level SAS file names refer to this SAS
data library. The default is USER=WORK, or USER=USER if the USER libref is
defined.

VERBOSE

Init. ON Writes a note in the log about system options set at initialization.

VNFERR

When a nonexistent input SAS dataset is required to contain a particular
variable: ON An error condition results. OFF The SAS dataset is treated
as containing the required variable.

WORK=

'*physical file name*' **Init.** The WORK library.

WORKINIT

Init. ON The WORK library is initialized at the beginning of the SAS
session. OFF The WORK library is not initialized.

WORKTERM

ON The WORK library is erased at the end of the SAS session.
OFF The WORK library is not erased.

YEARCUTOFF=

year The earliest year of the 100-year period that can be referred to with
two-digit year numbers by SAS date and SAS datetime informats, formats,
and functions.

LAST=

SAS dataset   Treated as the most recently created SAS dataset.

10

Macrolanguage

Macro objects are text objects that can be used to construct SAS statements and commands. *Macrolanguage* is a language that can be used to act on macro objects. You can use macrolanguage anywhere in a SAS program or on the command line.

Macrovariables

A *macrovariable* is a string of characters associated with a name.
You can assign a value to a macrovariable with the %LET statement or the SYMPUT routine. You refer to a macrovariable by using an ampersand (&) followed by the macrovariable name, optionally followed by a period:

&*name* or &*name*.

The period is necessary if the macrovariable reference is immediately followed by a letter, digit, underscore, or period.

In addition to the macrovariables you define, you can use references to the automatic macrovariables that are listed below. Those marked **(a)** can also be assigned new values in order to change the state of the session.

&SYSBUFFR	Extra text from %INPUT statement **(a)**
&SYSCMD	An unrecognized command from a macro window
&SYSDATE	The date when the SAS session started
&SYSDAY	The name of the day of the week when the SAS session started
&SYSDEVIC	Equivalent to the system option DEVICE= **(a)**
&SYSDSN	Characters 1–8: libref of the _LAST_ SAS dataset Characters 9–16: member name of the _LAST_ SAS dataset **(a)**
&SYSENV	FORE in foreground modes if TERMINAL system option is in effect, BACK otherwise
&SYSERR	The return code from a proc
&SYSFILRC	The error code from the FILENAME statement **(a)** **Release** 6.07+
&SYSINDEX	How many macros have started executing in the SAS session

&SYSINFO	Diagnostic information from some procs
&SYSJOBID	The user ID or job number of the SAS session
&SYSLAST	The _LAST_ SAS dataset **(a)**
&SYSFILRC	The error code from the LOCK statement **(a) Release** 6.07+
&SYSLIBRC	The error code from the LIBNAME statement **(a)**
&SYSMENV	S if a macro was invoked in a program D if a macro was invoked in a command
&SYSMSG	A message to be displayed in the message line of a macro window **(a)**
&SYSPARM	The parameter string from the SYSPARM= system option **(a)**
&SYSSCP	The operating system, abbreviated
&SYSTIME	The time of day when the SAS session started
&SYSVER	The SAS release number

Macro operators

The arithmetic, comparison, and logical operators can be used with macrovariables and other macro objects. The arithmetic operators work only with integer parts of values. The comparison operators do character comparisons, unless both operands are integers. Use the %EVAL function to evaluate a macro expression that uses macro operators, unless it appears as part of a macro statement.

Macro functions

Macro functions take one or more macro expressions as arguments and return a macro expression. Usually the returned value is a modified form of one of the arguments.

Some of these macro functions are actually implemented as macros in more recent SAS implementations. There is little practical difference between using a macro function and using a function-style macro.

%DATATYP

%DATATYP(*macro expression*)   Data type: returns NUMERIC for a numeric constant in regular or scientific notation, or CHAR otherwise.

%EVAL

%EVAL(*macro expression*)   Evaluates a macro expression that contains macro operators.

Macro quoting functions

The macro quoting functions modify the way the macro processor tokenizes and resolves a macro expression.

%STR(*macro expression*)   Quotes the unresolved macro expression, and treats it as constant text.

%NRSTR(*macro expression*)   Quotes the unresolved macro expression, treats it as constant text, and prevents it from being rescanned.

%QUOTE(*macro expression*)   Quotes the resolved macro expression.

%NRQUOTE(*macro expression*)   Quotes the resolved macro expression and prevents it from being rescanned.

%BQUOTE(*macro expression*)   Quotes the resolved macro expression and treats it as constant text.

%NRBQUOTE(*macro expression*)   Quotes the resolved macro expression, treats it as constant text, and prevents it from being rescanned.

%SUPERQ(*macrovariable name*)   A macrovariable reference: substitutes the value of the macrovariable and prevents it from being scanned.

%UNQUOTE(*macro expression*)   Unquotes: removes the effects of quoting functions.

Macro string functions

The macro string functions treat a macroexpression as a character string. They mostly correspond to the SAS functions of the same name.

%CMPRES(*string*)   Removes leading and trailing blanks and converts multiple blanks to single blanks.

%INDEX(*string, substring*)   Corresponds to INDEX function.

%LEFT(*string*)   Removes leading blanks.

%LENGTH(*string*)   Returns the actual length of the argument (including leading and trailing blanks, if quoted). Returns 0 for a null argument.

%LOWCASE(*string*)   Corresponds to LOWCASE function.
Release 6.07+

%SCAN(*string, n*)   %SCAN(*string, n, delimiters*)   Corresponds to SCAN function.

%SUBSTR(*string, start*)   %SUBSTR(*string, start, length*)   Corresponds to SUBSTR function.

%TRIM(*string*)   Removes trailing blanks.

%UPCASE(*string*)   Corresponds to UPCASE function.

%VERIFY(*string, characters*)   Corresponds to VERIFY function.

Macro string quoting functions

The macro string quoting functions duplicate macro string functions, except that they return a quoted result. The macro string functions, by contrast, always return an unquoted result.

%QCMPRES(*string*)

%QLEFT(*string*)

%QLOWCASE(*string*)   **Release** 6.07+

%QTRIM(*string*)

%QSCAN(*string, n*)   %QSCAN(*string, n, delimiters*)

%QSUBSTR(*string, start*)   %QSUBSTR(*string, start, length*)

%QUPCASE(*string*)

%SYSGET

%SYSGET(*variable or symbol name*)   Returns the value of the operating system variable or symbol.
Operating system UNIX, OS/2, VMS, Microsoft Windows

%SYSPROD

%SYSPROD(*name*)   Equivalent to the SYSPROD function. **Release** 6.07+

Macro statements

Macro statements are executed when the macro processor reaches them. Macro statements in macros are executed as the macro is resolved. Macro statements can appear just about anywhere in statements and commands in a SAS session.

%*

%* *text*;   Macro comment statement: no effect on session. Unlike the regular comment statement, a macro comment statement can appear anywhere a macro statement is allowed. Macro comment statements are not treated as part of a macro definition.

Macrolanguage references in macro comment statements are not resolved. (In a macro definition, regular comment statements are treated as constant text, and macrolanguage references in them are resolved as the macro is resolved.)

%DISPLAY

%DISPLAY *window or window.group options*;   Displays a macro window. In a macro, the window closes automatically when the macro ends. Outside a macro, the window closes automatically as soon as the user responds. **Options** BLANK BELL NOINPUT **Mode** Interactive

%DO . . . %END

%DO; *macro expression* %END;   Forms a macro block.

%DO %WHILE(*condition*) or %UNTIL(*condition*) or
macrovariable name = *start* %TO *stop* optional %BY *increment*;
macro expression %END;   Forms a macro loop, which is analogous to a data step DO loop. The macro expression is resolved repeatedly.
Use only in a macro definition.

%ELSE

%ELSE *macro expression*;   Immediately after an %IF . . . %THEN statement, it generates the macro expression if the %IF condition is false.
Use only in a macro definition.

%GLOBAL

%GLOBAL *macrovariable name* . . .;   Declares global macrovariables.

%GOTO

%GOTO *macro label*;   Branches to the macro label. The label must be in the same macro. A macro label has the form   %*label* :
Use only in a macro definition.

%IF . . . %THEN

%IF *condition* %THEN *macro expression* ;   Generates the macro expression only if the condition is true. **Use only in a macro definition.**

%INCLUDE

%INCLUDE *or* %INC *fileref or fileref(member) or 'physical file' . . . / options*; Includes the text file as part of the SAS program.

%INCLUDE *or* %INC *n or n–n or n:n / options*;   Repeats line(s) from earlier in the SAS session. **Mode** Interactive line mode

%INCLUDE *or* %INC *⋆*;   Includes lines typed by the user, until the user enters the %RUN statement. **Mode** Interactive line mode

Options

SOURCE2   Statements in the included file appear in the log.   NOSOURCE2 Statements in the included file do not appear in the log.

JCLEXCL   Excludes JCL lines. **Operating system** MVS

S2=*n*   Uses only the first *n* characters from each line in the file.

Example
%INC 'HERE.SAS';

%INPUT

%INPUT;   Reads the next program line into the automatic macrovariable SYSBUFFR.

%INPUT *macrovariable name* . . . ;   Reads the next program line into the macrovariable(s), and assigns any remaining words to the automatic macrovariable SYSBUFFR.

Mode Only useful in interactive line mode; valid only if &SYSENV=FORE

%KEYDEF

%KEYDEF *'function key name'*;   Writes the function-key definition in the log.

%KEYDEF *'function key name' 'command string' or command or ~ text*; Changes the definition of the function key.

%LET

%LET *macrovariable name* = *macro expression*;   Assigns a value to the macrovariable.

Examples
%LET I = 0;
%LET DAILY = %QUOTE(AMT = M(DAY)⋆RATE(DAY););

%LIST

%LIST *n or n–n or n:n / options*;   Lists the line or range of lines from earlier in the SAS session. **Mode** Interactive line mode

%LOCAL

%LOCAL *macrovariable name* ...; Declares local macrovariables. **Use only in a macro definition.**

%MACRO . . . %MEND

%MACRO *macro optional (parameters) / options; macro expression*
%MEND ...; Defines a macro. The macro expression is resolved when the macro is invoked. The parameters, if used, define local macrovariables that can be set when the macro is invoked.

Options

STMT Allows statement-style invocation.

CMD Allows command-style invocation. **Release** 6.07+

DES='*label*' Stores a description with the catalog entry. **Release** 6.07+

STORE Stores the compiled macro in the current macro catalog. **Release** 6.07+

PARMBUFF Assigns the parameter list, including parentheses, to the automatic macrovariable SYSPBUFF when the macro is called.

Example

```
%MACRO RESETP;
 PROC PRINTTO PRINT=PRINT;
RUN;
TITLE1 ' ';
FOOTNOTE;
OPTIONS PAGENO=1 NODATE NUMBER;
%MEND;
```

%PUT

%PUT *macro expression*; Writes the resolved macro expression in the log.

Example

```
%PUT SYSMENV IS &SYSMENV;
```

%RUN

%RUN; Ends the series of program lines that are typed by the user after a %INCLUDE * statement. Continues execution of the program.
Mode Interactive line mode

%SYSEXEC

%SYSEXEC; %SYSEXEC *command*; Equivalent to the X statement.
Mode Ignored in batch mode under some operating systems

%TSO

%TSO; %TSO *command*; Equivalent to the TSO statement.
Operating system MVS **Mode** Ignored in batch mode

%WINDOW

%WINDOW *window window options*
field definitions and/or group definitions;
Defines a macro window. The syntax of options, fields, and groups is the same as in the data step WINDOW statement, with these differences:

Informat/format specifications are not used. Instead, a number indicates the length of the field. Macrovariables, instead of data step variables, are displayed in variable fields.

Macros

A *macro* is a macro expression that is given a name and stored as a catalog entry of type MACRO. Macros are typically used to generate SAS statements that make up an entire SAS program or a part of a SAS program.

A macro is defined by the %MACRO and %MEND statements. After the macro is defined, it can be invoked by using its name preceded by a percent sign:

```
%MACRO macro;              %* macro definition;
macro expression
%MEND;
...

%macro                     %* macro invocation;
```

Often a macro has parameters, which are local macrovariables that can be given values when the macro is invoked. Parameters are listed in parentheses, separated by commas, after the macro name. In the %MACRO statement, the parameter names are given. In the macro invocation, values are given for the parameters.

There are two kinds of parameters. Positional parameters appear first in the list. Values for positional parameters must be supplied when the macro is invoked and must appear in the correct order. Keyword parameters can appear after the last positional parameter. In the %MACRO statement, the keyword parameter name is followed by an equals sign and a default value. In the macro invocation, a different value can optionally be supplied for the keyword parameter, using the same syntax. Keyword parameters can appear in any order at the end of the parameter list.

```
%MACRO macro(positional parameter name, ...,
             keyword parameter=default value, ...);
macro expression
%MEND;
...

%macro(positional parameter value, ...,
       keyword parameter name=value, ...)
```

In the macro, parameters are local macrovariables that can be used in the same way as any macrovariables.

Macros that are defined with the STMT option can also be invoked using a statement syntax:

```
macro  positional parameter value ...
       keyword parameter name=value ...;
```

Command-style invocation works about the same way, but it allows a macro to be used as a command in a display manager window.

When the MAUTOSOURCE system option is in effect, a set of macros can be used in a program without having to be defined in the same program. Each autocall macro is defined in a separate member of an autocall library, which is a library of SAS programs that is identified by the SASAUTOS= system option. The SAS System also provides a set of utility macros.

Example

These macro statements define the macro CLOSE with positional and keyword parameters:

```
%MACRO CLOSE(X1, X2, TOL=.00001);
  (ABS((&X1) - (&X2)) <= ABS(&TOL))
%MEND;
```

Later, the macro can be called with values supplied for the positional parameters and, optionally, the keyword parameter:

```
%CLOSE(THICK, 2.0072, TOL=.0002)
```

The macro processor

The *macro processor* intercepts programs lines and command lines in a SAS session and resolves macrolanguage references. It scans the incoming text and does the following:

- executes macro statements
- substitutes values for macrovariables, macros, and macro functions
- deletes macro comment statements
- converts double ampersands to single ampersands

It then rescans any text generated from macro objects, and repeats the process until no macrolanguage references remain.

Macrolanguage references are not resolved inside constants that are enclosed in single quotes, but are resolved in constants that are enclosed in double quotes.

Examples

The scanning examples below use these macrovariables and macro:

```
%LET LA = 6;
%LET LETTER = L;
%MACRO A(X); MISSING %UPCASE(&X) %LOWCASE(&X); %MEND;
```

When the macro processor scans this text:

```
&&&LETTER.A..4
```

it converts && to & and &LETTER. to L:

&LA..4

On rescanning, the text resolves to:

6.4

Scanning works the same way when macros and macro functions are involved. This reference:

%&LETTER(A B C D E)

becomes:

%A(A B C D E)

MISSING %UPCASE(&X) %LOWCASE(&X);

MISSING %UPCASE(A B C D E) %LOWCASE(A B C D E);

MISSING A B C D E a b c d e;

11

Files

Files are declared in FILENAME and LIBNAME statements and then used in data step and proc step statements.

Devices

In addition to physical files, the SAS System's file routines also handle a few kinds of devices, which are identified by special device names.

DISK	On-line storage
DUMMY	Nothing
NAMEPIPE	Named pipe **Operating system** OS/2
PIPE	Unnamed pipe **Operating system** OS/2, UNIX
PLOTTER	Plotter
PRINTER	Printer
TAPE	Sequential storage
TERMINAL	Line-mode user I/O

Libraries

A SAS data library is either a physical file or a directory, depending on the operating system. Each library is identified by a different name, or *libref*. The librefs that are listed below have specific meanings in a SAS session.

SASUSER	Characteristics of the interactive user, including the user profile
WORK	Short-term storage within a SAS session; one-level SAS dataset names refer to this library by default
USER	One-level SAS dataset names refer to this library if it is defined
SASHELP	Help windows; sample data
LIBRARY	Add-on informats and formats

Engines

Access to SAS libraries is mediated by routines called *engines*. There is a *native engine* for each release of the SAS System. There are also *transport engines*, which store SAS files in an ASCII text format so that they can be moved betweeen SAS implementations, and *interface engines*, which create or access files in formats defined by other software systems.

These are some examples of native library engines:

V607 V606 V5 V606SEQ V5SEQ XPORT REMOTE

These are some interface engines:

BMDP OSIRIS SPSS CDD DTIF

The ENGINE= system option determines which native library engine is used by default. You can specify the engine for a new SAS data library immediately after the libref in the LIBNAME statement.

Member types

The SAS files that are members of a SAS data library are identified by two-level names of the form *libref.member*. The SAS files can belong to several different member types. Sometimes, within a SAS data library, a member is identified by a two-level name of the form *member.type*, to distinguish members of different types that have the same name. These are the member types:

DATA	SAS data file
VIEW	SAS data view
CATALOG	SAS catalog
PROGRAM	Compiled data step
ACCESS	Access descriptor

Entry types

A SAS catalog contains data structures that are called *entries*. There are many different entry types, each with a specific purpose. In a SAS program, an entry is usually identified by a four-level name, *libref.catalog.entry.type*. Within a particular catalog, an entry can be identified by a two level name, *entry.type*. In some contexts, the entry type can be omitted, for a one-level name.

These are the entry types:

AFGO	Identifies the AF entry recently displayed
AFPGM	Values that are entered on a program entry window
CALC	Spreadsheet
CBT	AF window with text and questions and answers

DICTNARY	Spelling dictionary
EDPARMS	Editing environment in BUILD or FSLETTER proc
FONT	Font
FORM	Page setup for printing
FORMAT	Numeric format
FORMATC	Character format
FORMULA	Window definition for FSVIEW proc
FRAME	AF window that is defined using objects
GLOBAL	SYMBOL, LEGEND, AXIS, or PATTERN statement
GOPTIONS	Graphics options
GRSEG	Graphics output
HELP	AF window that displays text
INFMT	Numeric informat
INFMTC	Character informat
KEYS	A set of function key definitions
LETTER	Letter (often a form letter) in FSLETTER proc
LIST	A list of values that are used for data validation
LOG	Text from the LOG window
MACRO	Macro
MENU	AF window allowing menu selection
MSYMTAB	Values of local macrovariables
OUTPUT	Text from the OUTPUT window
PARMS	Spreadsheet defaults
PGM	Spreadsheet program
PMENU	Menu bar
PROFILE	User characteristics
PROGRAM	AF window that contains an SCL program
REPORT	Spreadsheet report layout
REPT	Report design for REPORT proc
SCL	SCL program with no window
SCREEN	Window definition for FSEDIT proc
SLIST	SCL list
SOURCE	Text from text editor window
TITLE	Title line or footnote line
TRANTAB	Translation table
WSAVE	Window size and location

Special SAS dataset names

These special SAS dataset names can be used in most places where the syntax of a SAS statement or command calls for a SAS dataset name.

ALL   In some contexts, all the SAS datasets in a library

DATA   The next in the series DATA1, DATA2, DATA3, . . .

LAST   The most recently created SAS dataset

NULL   No SAS dataset

Views

A *view*, or SAS data view, is a SAS dataset that is physically stored in two or more files. Typically, the data description is stored in one or two files and the data values are stored in one or more different files.

Views that use data values in SAS datasets can be created in the SQL proc or in the data step. SQL views are defined using SQL query syntax. Data step views are created by adding the VIEW= option to the DATA statement of a data step. The data values in both SQL views and data step views are not determined until a later step reads from the view; then the values are put together one observation at a time. Thus, the data values in a view can be changed by changing the data values in the files that the view refers to.

A data step view can also create a SAS dataset from data in an input text file or from any other source of data available to the data step.

Passwords

Beginning with SAS release 6.07, SAS files other than catalogs can be protected by passwords. Operations on SAS files are divided into these categories, or levels:

ALTER
WRITE
READ

You can have separate passwords for different levels of access, or the same password for all access to the file. You can password-protect all levels or only the higher levels; for example, an alter-protected file can be written and read without a password. Higher-level passwords can be used in place of lower-level passwords: an ALTER password can be used to write or read a file, or a WRITE password can be used to read a file.

For SAS datasets, passwords are mainly implemented using dataset options. The READ=, WRITE=, and ALTER= dataset options are used for different levels of password protection, or the PW= dataset option for a single password. Use the dataset option to assign the password when you create the SAS file. Later, use the same password when you read, write, or alter the SAS dataset. You can change, add, or remove passwords for existing SAS datasets using the DATASETS proc.

For compiled data steps, passwords are used with options, which look like dataset options, after the PGM= option in the DATA statement.

In display manager, passwords can be added and changed interactively in the ACCESS window. If you do not supply a password or supply an incorrect password for a protected file in a display manager session, a requestor window prompts you for the correct password.

When you create a file, you can assign the same password for all three levels using the PW= option. You can then use the PW= option or one of the other password options when accessing that file. The PW= option can also be used with the appropriate password when accessing an file that has different passwords for different levels.

Passwords are used with these syntax rules:

Assigning passwords when creating a file:
  password option=password ...

Accessing a protected file:
  password option=password

Adding a password to an existing file:
  password option=/password

Removing a password:
  password option=password /
  ALTER=*password password option=/*

Removing the READ password from a file that is write-protected but not alter-protected:
  WRITE=*password* READ=*password/*

Changing a password:
  password option=old password /new password
  ALTER=*password password option=/new password*

Changing the READ password of a file that is write-protected but not alter-protected:
  WRITE=*password* READ=*old password /new password*

12

Descriptive statistics

A *statistic* is a number that is calculated from a statistical sample or population. The SAS System has special support for a group of *descriptive statistics*. For the most part, they are simple, general statistics that can be used to describe any set of data.

Statistics programming

The descriptive statistics can be calculated in a data step or in various procs. In a data step, you can use a set of variables as a population to calculate a statistic. Use the variables as arguments to the function whose name is the name of the statistic.

In a proc that supports descriptive statistics, you can calculate a statistic on all the values of a single variable in a SAS dataset. Name the statistic and variables in the PROC, OUTPUT, or other statement, according to the syntax rules of the proc.

The VARDEF= option on the PROC statement and the optional FREQ and WEIGHT statements affect the way the proc calculates the statistics. The VARDEF= option can have one of four values:

N	population statistics
DF	sample statistics
WGT *or* WEIGHT	weighted population statistics
WDF	weighted sample statistics

The value you specify in the VARDEF= option controls the divisor that is used to calculate the variance and indirectly affects many other statistics.

The optional WEIGHT statement names a weight variable, which indicates the relative importance, or weight, of each observation. Fractional values are allowed for the weight variable. Usually, you want to treat each observation as equally important, so you would not use a weight variable.

If the value of the weight variable in an observation is less than 0 or is missing, a weight of 0 is used for that observation.

The FREQ statement names a frequency variable, which indicates the number of times an observation should be used. For example, if the value of the frequency variable is 3 in an observation in the SAS dataset, that observation represents three observations with the same values.

Statistics

Some of the more complicated descriptive statistics, marked **S** in the entries below, are not implemented as functions and are available only in selected procs.

Many statistics are meaningful only for certain kinds of samples. The specific requirements are noted in the entries below.

You can also calculate the statistics directly from the sample values or from other statistics. The formulas are shown in the entries that follow. These additional symbols are used in the formulas:

D	The variance divisor: N, if VARDEF=N or when using functions $N - 1$, if VARDEF=DF SUMWGT, if VARDEF=WGT SUMWGT $- 1$, if VARDEF=WDF
x	Each of the values in the sample
w	Each of the weights (1, if the sample is unweighted)
Σ	Summation over the values in the sample
SC	Σx^3
SF	Σx^4
MEAN^2	MEAN$\star$MEAN
MEAN^3	MEAN$\star$MEAN$\star$MEAN
VAR^2	VAR$\star$VAR

CSS

Corrected sum of squares. Sum of squares, corrected for the mean.
Formula USS – MEAN$\star$SUM   **Requires** $N \geq 1$

CV

Percent coefficient of variation.   **Formula** 100$\star$STD/MEAN
Requires $N \geq 2$, MEAN $\neq 0$

KURTOSIS

Kurtosis. A measurement of the importance of the extreme areas (tail thickness) of the distribution.
Formula (SF – 4$\star$MEAN$\star$SC + 6$\star$MEAN$^2 \star$USS – 3$\star$MEAN$^3 \star$SUM)/(VAR^2)
$\star$N$\star$(N + 1)/((N – 1)$\star$(N – 2) $\star$(N – 3)) – 3$\star$(N – 1)^2/((N – 2)$\star$(N – 3))
Requires $N \geq 4$, STD $\neq 0$, unweighted

MAX

Maximum. The highest value.

MEAN

Mean. The arithmetic average of the values.   **Formula** SUM/SUMWGT

MIN

Minimum. The lowest value.

MODE
S The most common value.

N
Sample size; number of nonmissing values.

NMISS
Number of missing values.

PRT
S The two-tailed probability value for T.   **Formula** $2*PROBT(-ABS(T), N - 1)$
Requires $N \geq 2$, STD $\neq 0$

Quantiles
S Values that are selected so that a certain relative frequency is above the value and a certain relative frequency is below. In particular, the median is in the middle, with half the values above it and half below it.

RANGE
Range. The difference between the maximum and minimum.
Formula $MAX - MIN$

SKEWNESS
Skewness. A measurement of the sidedness of the distribution.   **Formula**
$(SC - 3*MEAN*USS + 2*MEAN^2*SUM)/(VAR*STD)*N/((N - 1)*(N - 2))$
Requires $N \geq 3$, STD $\neq 0$, unweighted

STD
Standard deviation. The square root of the variance. A measure of dispersion.   **Formula** $SQRT(VAR)$ **Requires** $N \geq 2$

STDERR
Standard error of the mean.   **Formula** $SQRT(VAR/N)$ **Requires** $N \geq 2$

SUM
Sum. Total.   **Formula** $\sum wx$

SUMWGT
S Sum of weights. In an unweighted sample, N.   **Formula** $\sum w$

T
Student's t statistic. Used to test the null hypothesis that the mean of the population that the sample represents is 0.   **Formula** $MEAN/STDERR$
Requires $N \geq 2$, STD $\neq 0$

USS
Uncorrected sum of squares.   **Formula** $\sum wx^2$

VAR
Variance.   **Formula** CSS/D **Requires** $D > 0$

13

Display manager

Display manager is the usual interactive environment of the SAS System, which appears when you invoke the SAS System with the DMS system option in effect. Display manager displays several windows simultaneously. Different windows have different purposes and uses. The windows can overlap and can be moved and resized.

Using windows

Some actions work the same way in most or all display manager windows.

Parts of a window

These window parts are not used all the time or in every window, but they have the same function in every window where they appear.

Border
: A rectangle around the outside of the window. In some operating systems, you can change the size of the window by dragging the border.

Name
: The name of the window often appears in the top border, sometimes called the *title bar*. In some operating systems, you can move the window by dragging the title bar.

Command line
: A line directly below the top border of the window in which you can type commands.

Menu bar
: A line directly below the top border of the window that contains options, usually commands, that you can select. The menu bar takes the place of the command line.

Pull-down menu
: A vertically oriented menu that sometimes appears when you select a menu item.

Message line
: A line directly below the command line or menu bar, in which messages appear. The messages include error messages when the syntax of a command is incorrect.

Scroll bars
: Bars along the side or bottom of a window that allow you to move through data that is too long or wide to fit in the window.

Window states

The actions you can take in a window depend on what state the window is in. You can usually tell a window's state by its appearance.

Inactive   The window is open, but is not the front window. If the window is visible, you can activate the window by pointing to it.

Active   The window is the front window, taking up part or all of the screen. You can work in the window, move it, resize it, zoom it, or icon it.

Zoomed   The window takes up the entire screen. You can work in the window or icon it.

Iconed   The window shrinks to a symbol the size of a postage stamp. You can activate it by pointing.

Display manager windows

Each display manager window has a different purpose and is used in a particular way.

ACCESS

Lists the members of active SAS data libraries.
Command to activate ACCESS **Release** 6.07+

Window commands

COPY *libref.member or libref.member.type* *libref or libref.member or libref.member.type* Copies a SAS file.

EXTRACT *SAS dataset SAS data file*   Creates a SAS data file with the data from a view (or other SAS dataset).

LABEL   Displays or removes a column of SAS dataset labels.

LIBRARY   Displays a message that shows the current libref.

LIBRARY *libref*   Displays only members of the library named.

LIBRARY _ALL_   Displays members of all active libraries.

MEMTYPE   Displays a message that shows the current member type.

MEMTYPE *member type*   Displays only members of the type specified.

MEMTYPE _ALL_   Displays members of all types.

REPLACE *libref.member or libref.member.type or SAS data file name libref.name or libref.name.type or name*   Duplicates a SAS file and gives the copy the indicated new name . If a file already exists with the new name, it is replaced.

SORT LIBNAME *or* NAME *or* MEMTYPE . . .   Changes the order of rows in the window.

Selection codes

?   Displays a popup menu.

B   Displays the SAS dataset using the FSBROWSE proc (if the proc is installed).

BL   Displays the SAS dataset using the FSVIEW proc (if the proc is installed).

C   Opens the CONTENTS window or catalog directory window.

D   Deletes the entry.

E   Displays the SAS dataset for editing using the FSEDIT proc (if the proc is installed).

EL   Displays the SAS dataset for editing using the FSVIEW proc (if the proc is installed).

PW   Allows you to add, change, or remove passwords.

R   Allows the member name and description to be changed.

AF

Displays an AF application. **Command to activate** AF

Window commands

PREVIEW   Opens the preview window to allow the preview buffer to be edited.

SELECT   Selects the field at the cursor position for copying.
REPEAT   Copies the selected field to the field at the cursor position.

WREGION *top left height width* or TOP or LEFT or RIGHT or BOTTOM or TOP DEVICE or LEFT DEVICE or RIGHT DEVICE or BOTTOM DEVICE   Sets the location and size of the next window to be opened.

WREGION CLEAR   Resets the location and size of the next window to be opened.

AFA

The same as the AF window, except that a separate AFA window is opened for each separate application. **Command to activate** AFA **Release 6.07+**

APPOINTMENT

Displays a calendar and allows a SAS dataset of appointments to be edited. **Command to activate** APPOINTMENT

Window actions Select a day by pointing to it. You can then edit the list of appointments for that day. Changes are saved immediately to the SAS dataset. Display a different month by scrolling vertically or typing a different year and month.

Window commands

CLEAR   Erases the day's appointments.

DELETE   Erases the appointment at the cursor location.

ATTRIBUTES

Describes a SAS dataset. **Action to activate** Button in CONTENTS window **Window actions** Type over values. **Release 6.07+**

CALCULATOR

Acts like a desktop calculator. **Command to activate** CALCULATOR

Window actions Type numbers and operators to be calculated. Type = and press the enter key to get a result.

CATALOG

Lists entries in a catalog. **Command to activate** CATALOG, or the S or X selection code in the DIR window

Window actions Type over the libref and catalog to display a different catalog.

Selection codes

? Displays a popup menu. **Release** 6.07+

D Deletes the entry.

R Allows the entry name and description to be changed.

S *or* X Opens an OUTPUT, LOG, or SOURCE window for editing in the NOTEPAD window.

CONTENTS

Describes variables of a SAS dataset. **Command to activate** C selection code in ACCESS window **Release** 6.07+

Window actions For a SAS data file, type over variable names and attributes to change them. Press the Attributes button to open the ATTRIBUTES window.

Window commands

SORT NAME Displays variables in name order.

SORT SORT ORDER Displays variables in position order.

INDEX CREATE Opens the INDEX CREATE window.

INDEX REVIEW Opens the INDEX REVIEW window.

DIR

Lists members in a library. **Command to activate** DIR, or the S or X selection code in the LIBNAME window

Window actions Type over the libref to display a different library. Type a value in the type field to display a particular member type, or type ALL to display all members.

Selection codes

? Displays a popup menu. **Release** 6.07+

B Displays the SAS dataset using the FSVIEW proc (if the proc is installed). **Release** 6.06+

D Deletes the member. **Release** 6.06+

R Allows the member name to be changed.

S *or* X Opens a VAR window for a SAS dataset or a CATALOG window for a catalog.

DSINFO

Describes a file. **Command to activate** DSINFO, or the X selection code in the FNAME window **Operating system** MVS

FILENAME

Displays all defined filerefs and their physical file names.
Command to activate FILENAME

FNAME

Lists librefs and filerefs. **Command to activate** FNAME
Operating system MVS

Selection codes

%   Submits the sequential file to be executed as SAS statements.

B   Opens a browse window for the sequential file.

C   Opens the MEMLIST window for the fileref.

E   Opens an edit window for the sequential file.

F   Frees (releases) the file.

I   Copies the sequential file to the PROGRAM EDITOR window and activates that window.

M   Opens the MEMLIST window for the physical PDS.

X   Opens a DSINFO window for the file.

FOOTNOTES

Displays footnote lines for editing. **Command to activate** FOOTNOTES

Window commands

CANCEL   Closes the window and restores previous footnote lines.

END   Closes the window normally.

FORM

Displays a FORM entry for editing. **Command to activate** FSFORM

Window commands

=1   =2   =3   =4   =5   NEXTSCR   PREVSCR   Displays the different panels of the window.

DES   Displays the FORM entry's description.

DES *description*   Changes the FORM entry's description.

SPRINT *options*   Prints the window as currently displayed. **Options** NOBORDER FILE=*file* FORM=*form* **Release** 6.07+

SPRINT FREE   Frees the SPRINT print file. **Release** 6.07+

HELP

Displays a SAS System help window. **Command to activate** HELP

Window actions Scroll if necessary. View additional help windows by pointing to selected words and phrases.

INDEX CREATE

Allows you to create indexes for a SAS data file.
Command to activate INDEX CREATE in the CONTENTS window
Window actions Enter the required information and then the RUN command to create an index. **Release** 6.07+

Window commands

RUN   Creates the index.

REVIEW   Opens the INDEX REVIEW window.

INDEX REVIEW

Lists indexes of a SAS data file. **Command to activate** REVIEW in the INDEX CREATE window or INDEX REVIEW in the CONTENTS window
Release 6.07+

Selection code

D   Deletes an index.

KEYS

Displays function key definitions for editing. **Command to activate** KEYS

Window commands

CANCEL   Closes the window and restores the previously saved or default function key definitions.

COPY   Replaces the contents of the window with the function key definitions from the user profile.

COPY *entry*   Replaces the contents of the window with the function key definitions from the KEYS entry.

END   Closes the window and saves any changes in the user profile.

SAVE   Saves changes in the user profile.

SAVE *entry*   Saves changes in a KEYS entry.

LIBNAME

Displays all defined librefs and their engines and physical file names.
Command to activate LIBNAME

Selection codes

?   Displays a popup menu. **Release** 6.07+

S *or* X   Opens a DIR window for the library.

LOG

Displays the log. **Command to activate** LOG

Window commands

AUTOSCROLL   Displays the window's automatic scrolling increment.

AUTOSCROLL *distance*   Sets the window's automatic scrolling increment.
AUTOSCROLL 0   Turns off automatic scrolling.

LINESIZE   Displays the log's line size.

LINESIZE *n*   Sets the log's line size.

MEMLIST

Lists the members of a PDS. **Command to activate** MEMLIST, or the C or M selection codes in the FNAME window **Operating system** MVS

Selection codes

%   Submits the PDS member to be executed as SAS statements.

B, S   Opens a browse window for the PDS member.

D   Deletes the PDS member.

E   Opens an edit window for the PDS member.

I   Copies the PDS member to the PROGRAM EDITOR window and activates that window.

R   Renames the PDS member.

NOTEPAD

Displays text from a SOURCE, LOG, or OUTPUT entry for editing.
Command to activate NOTEPAD, or the S or X selection code in the
CATALOG window **Window actions** Text editing.

Window commands

DESCRIPTION   Displays the entry's description.

DESCRIPTION *description*   Changes the entry's description.

NTITLE *'description'*   Changes the window's title.

CANCEL   Closes the window and discards changes.

END   Closes the window and saves changes.

OPTIONS

Displays selected system options for editing.
Command to activate OPTIONS

Window commands

CANCEL   Closes the window and restores previous values for the system
options.

END   Closes the window normally.

OUTPUT

Displays the standard print file. **Command to activate** OUTPUT, LISTING,
or the S or X selection code in the OUTPUT MANAGER window

Window commands

AUTOSCROLL   Displays the window's scrolling increment.

AUTOSCROLL *distance*   Sets the window's automatic scrolling increment.
AUTOSCROLL 0   Turns off automatic scrolling.

LINESIZE   Displays the standard print file's line size.

LINESIZE *n*   Sets the standard print file's line size.

PAGE *toggle*   Displays paged or unpaged text.

PAGESIZE   Displays the standard print file's page size.

PAESIZE *n*   Sets the standard print file's line size.

OUTPUT MANAGER

Displays a list of program steps that have produced print output.
Command to activate OUTPUT or MANAGER **Release 6.06+**

Selection codes

?   Displays a popup menu. **Release 6.07+**

B   Displays the step's output in a text editor window for browsing.

D   Deletes the step's output.

E   Displays the step's output in a text editor window for editing. (In that
window, you can use the REPLACE command to store your changes in
the standard print file.)

F   Stores the step's output in a separate print file.

O   Stores the step's output in a catalog entry.

P   Prints the step's output.

R   Allows the description of the step to be changed.

S *or* X   Displays the step's output in the OUTPUT window.

PROGRAM EDITOR

A text editor window.   **Command to activate** PROGRAM
Window actions Text editing.

Window commands

RECALL   RECALL *n*   Retrieves a previously submitted block of lines.

SUBMIT   SUB   END   Submits the contents of the window to be executed
as SAS statements. (**Release** 6.07+: If text is marked in the window, only
the marked text is submitted.)

SUBMIT *'statements'*   Submits the specified string to be executed.

SUBMIT BUF=*buffer*   Submits a named paste buffer. **Release** 6.07+

SUBTOP   SUBTOP *n*   Submits the first line or first lines from the window
to be executed.

SETINIT

Displays information about the SAS installation.
Command to activate SETINIT

SITEINFO

Displays identifying information about the SAS site.
Command to activate SITEINFO

TITLES

Displays title lines for editing.   **Command to activate** TITLES
Window commands

CANCEL   Closes the window and restores previous title lines.

END   Closes the window normally.

VAR

Lists the variables in a SAS dataset, with the variables' attributes.
Command to activate VAR, or the S or X selection code in the DIR window

Window actions Type over the libref and member name to see a different
SAS dataset.

Selection codes

?   Displays a popup menu. **Release** 6.07+

R   Allows the variable's name, informat, format, and label attributes to be
changed.

Commands

Both display manager and text editor commands are listed here. A
command can be entered by typing it on the command line, by selecting it
from a pull-down menu, or by pressing a function key that is defined as

that command. To execute a command in a SAS program, use the DM statement.

Not all commands are valid in all windows. Text editor commands can be used only in text editor windows. Text editor editing commands cannot be used in browse windows.

Text editor *line commands* are also listed here. Line commands are normally entered in the line number fields of a text editor window. They can be entered on the command line or in a function key, prefixed by a colon (:). A *block command* is a line command that affects a block of lines. Enter the block command on the first and last lines of the block.

An argument for a line command should immediately follow the line command, with no blanks in between. The arguments are optional, with a default of 1, except as indicated. The argument for a block command only needs to be entered on one of the two lines that define the block.

Many display manager and text editor commands are *mode-toggle* commands. The syntax of all mode-toggle commands is the same:

mode ON   Turns the mode on.
mode OFF   Turns the mode off.
mode   Switches the mode between on and off.

Scrolling commands use a standard set of options to represent scrolling distances:

n   A specific number of lines or columns.
CURSOR   CUR   C   To the cursor location.
HALF   H   Half the height or width of the window.
MAX   M   To the end of the data.
PAGE   P   The height or width of the window.

(

Line command (*n*   **Block command** ((*n*   Shifts left *n* columns, deleting the first *n* characters.

)

Line command)*n*   **Block command**))*n*   Shifts right *n* columns.

<

Line command <*n*   **Block command** <<*n*   Shifts left *n* columns, but does not delete nonblank characters.

=X

=X   Closes all help windows or an AF application. **Alias** QCAN

>

Line command >*n*   **Block command** >>*n*   Shifts right *n* columns, but does not delete nonblank characters.

?

?   Restores the previously entered command line. **Alias for** PREVCMD *n*

n   Scrolls to the indicated line.

A

Line command A   Indicates that text is to be copied after this line.

ACCESS

ACCESS ACCESS *libref*   Activates the ACCESS window.
Release 6.07+

AF

AF *options*   Opens an AF application in the AF window.
Options
C=*entry*   Identifies the AF entry to be displayed.

FRAME=*name or number*   Selects a frame of a CBT entry.

n   Selects an option from a MENU entry.

AFA

AFA *options*   Opens an AF application in its own AFA window.
Alias for AFAPPL **Release** 6.07+

APPOINTMENT

APPOINTMENT *options*   Opens the APPOINTMENT window.
Alias APPT
Options
SAS dataset   Identifies the appointment dataset to be displayed.

two-letter weekday abbreviation   Selects the day to be displayed.

B   Opens in browse mode.

AUTOADD

AUTOADD *toggle*   **Mode**   On: displays blank lines when you scroll past
the bottom of the text in a text editor window. Off: displays END OF TEXT
at the bottom of the text in a text editor window.

AUTOFLOW

AUTOFLOW *toggle*   **Mode**   On: flows text imported with the INCLUDE,
COPY or PASTE command.

AUTOPOP

AUTOPOP *toggle*   **Mode**   On: activates the window automatically when
its contents change.

AUTOSPLIT

AUTOSPLIT *toggle*   **Mode**   Controls what happens when you press the
enter key in the middle of a line of text in a text editor window. On: splits
the line of text into two lines. Off: moves the cursor the the beginning of
the next line.

AUTOWRAP

AUTOWRAP *toggle* **Mode** Controls what happens when data that is wider than the window is imported with the INCLUDE or COPY command or when data is stored with the FILE command to a file that is narrower than the data. On: wraps text. Off: truncates text.

B

Line command B Indicates that text is to be copied before this line.

BACKWARD

BACKWARD BACKWARD *distance* Scrolls up. **Alias** UP, BAC

BFIND

BFIND *'string' part option* Searches backward for a string. Equivalent to the FIND command with the PREV option.

BOTTOM

BOTTOM Scrolls down to the bottom.

BOUNDS

BOUNDS Indicates the current left and right boundaries in a text editor window. The boundaries control text flow and alignment.
BOUNDS *left right* Sets new left and right boundaries.

BYE

BYE Ends the SAS session. **Alias** ENDSAS

C

Line command C*n* **Block command** CC Copies lines to the location that is indicated by the A, B, or O line command.

CALCULATOR

CALCULATOR Activates the CALCULATOR window.
Alias DCALCULATOR, DCALC, CALCU

CANCEL

CANCEL Closes a window immediately. In some windows, this discards or undoes changes. **Alias** CAN

CAPS

CAPS *toggle* **Mode** On: converts any lowercase letters that you type to uppercase letters.

CASCADE

CASCADE Cascades all open windows so that the names are visible.

CATALOG

CATALOG CATALOG *catalog* Activates the CATALOG window.
Alias CAT

CHANGE

CHANGE *'string' 'string' options*   Searches for the first string and replaces it with the second string.

CHANGE   Repeats the search and replacement of the most recent CHANGE command.

Options The same as those used in the FIND command.   **Alias** C
Example CHANGE '¬' '^' ALL

CL

Line command CL*n*   **Block command** CCL   Changes letters to lowercase.

CLEAR

CLEAR   CLEAR *window*   Clears the data area of the window.

CLEAR *part*   Clears the indicated part of the window. Parts include TEXT, MASK, and TABS.

CLEAR RECALL   Clears the recall buffer so that previously submitted lines cannot be recalled.

Alias CLE

CLOCK

CLOCK *toggle*   **Mode**   On: displays the time in the bottom line of the screen. **Operating system** MVS

COLOR

COLOR *part color optional video attribute*   Sets the color and video attribute of a part of the window.

Parts
BACKGROUND BAC Background
BANNER BAN The protected part of the command line
BORDER BO Border
BYLINE Line that shows BY variables in OUTPUT window
COMMAND COM Command line or menu items
DATA DA Data lines in LOG or OUTPUT window
ERROR E Error messages in LOG window
FOOTNOTE Footnote lines in OUTPUT window
HEADER Header lines in OUTPUT window
MENU Background for pull-down menus
MENUBORDER MENUB Menu borders
MESSAGE MES MSG Message line
MTEXT MT Marked text
NOTES NO Notes in LOG window
NUMBERS NUMB Line numbers
SOURCE SO Source lines in LOG window
TEXT TE Text
TITLE Title lines in OUTPUT window
WARNING WA Warning messages in LOG window

Colors RED R GREEN G BLUE B CYAN C MAGENTA M YELLOW Y BLACK K GRAY GREY A WHITE W NEXT

Video attributes REVERSE R BLINK B HIGHLIGHT H UNDERLINE U

COLS

Line command COLS   Displays a ruler. **Alias** CO

COMMAND

COMMAND *toggle*   **Mode**   On: displays a menu bar or a command line in the window, depending on the PMENU mode.
Off: displays a command line in the window. **Alias** COM

COPY

COPY *entry options*   Copies the catalog entry into the window.

COPY *entry entry*   Duplicates an entry.

Options When copying into a text editor window, all the options of the INCLUDE command apply.

CU

Line command CU*n*   **Block command** CCU   Changes letters to uppercase.

CURSOR

CURSOR   Moves the cursor to the command line. **Alias** CUR

CUT

CUT *options*   Cuts marked text from the window and copies it to a paste buffer. Options are the same as those used in the STORE command.

D

Line command D*n*   **Block command** DD   Deletes lines.

DELETE

DELETE *entry*   Deletes a catalog entry. **Alias** DEL

DICT

DICT CREATE *dictionary optional size in bytes*   Creates a new dictionary.

DICT INCLUDE *dictionary*   Opens a dictionary.

DICT FREE *dictionary*   Closes a dictionary. Saves changes, if it is a user dictionary.

Release 6.06+

DIR

DIR   DIR *libref*   DIR *libref.member type*   Activates a DIR window.

DSINFO

DSINFO *fileref or libref or 'physical file name'*   Activates the DSINFO window. **Operating system** MVS

DOWN

DOWN   DOWN *distance*   Scrolls down. **Alias** DO **Alias for** FORWARD

END

END   Closes a window normally. **Alias** SUBMIT, SUB

ENDSAS

ENDSAS   Ends the SAS session. **Alias for** BYE

FILE

FILE *file options*   Stores the window's text data in a text file.

FILE   Stores the window's text data in the text file most recently used in a FILE or INCLUDE statement.

Options

APPEND A Appends to the file.
REPLACE R Replaces the previous contents of the file.

TABS T Compresses the file by replacing blanks with tabs.

ATTR Also stores attributes along with the text.

FILENAME

FILENAME   Activates the FILENAME window.   **Alias** FILEN

FILL

FILL   FILL *'character' and/or n*   If the cursor is in a text field in a text editor window, it inserts *n* fill characters at the cursor location.

Example
FILL '-' 80

FIND

FIND *'string' options*   Searches for the string.

FIND   Repeats the most recent text search.

Options
Where: NEXT N Forward from the cursor location.   FIRST F Forward from the beginning of text.   PREV Backward from the cursor location. LAST L Backward from the end of text.   ALL A All occurrences in the text.

Part: PREFIX PREF At beginning of word.   SUFFIX SUF At end of word.   WORD W As entire word.

ICASE Ignores case: treats uppercase and lowercase letters as matching. **Release** 6.07+

Alias F

FNAME

FNAME   Activates the FNAME window. **Operating system** MVS

FOOTNOTES

FOOTNOTES   Activates the FOOTNOTES window.
Alias FOOT, FOOTNOTE

FORMNAME

FORMNAME   Displays the name of the current form (for printing).

FORMNAME *form or* CLEAR   Changes the form.

FORWARD

FORWARD   FORWARD *distance*   Scrolls down. **Alias** FORW, DOWN, DO

FREE

FREE   Closes the print file.

FSFORM

FSFORM *entry*   Activates the FSFORM window to edit the indicated FORM entry.

HELP

HELP   HELP *word*   Opens a help window.

HOME

HOME   Moves the cursor to the command line. **Alias** HO

HSCROLL

HSCROLL *distance*   Sets the default horizontal scrolling distance. **Alias** HS

I

Line command I*n*   IA*n*   Inserts lines after the current line.

Line command IB*n*   Inserts lines before the current line.

ICON

ICON *toggle*   **Mode**   On: it shrinks the window to an icon.

INCLUDE

INCLUDE *fileref or 'physical file name' options*   Copies the text file into the text editor window.

INCLUDE   Copies the text file most recently used in a FILE or INCLUDE command into the text editor window.

Options

NOATTR   Does not copy attributes that are stored in the text file.

NOTABS   Converts tabs to blanks.

REPLACE   R   Replaces the contents of the window.

Alias INC

INDENT

INDENT *toggle*   **Mode**   On: keeps lines indented when flowing text. Off: left-aligns when flowing text.

JC

Line command JC   **Block command** JJC   Centers the line between the left and right boundaries.

Line command JC*n*   **Block command** JJC*n*   Centers the line around the *n*th column.

JL

Line command JL   **Block command** JJL   Left-aligns the line at the left boundary.

Line command JL*n*   **Block command** JJL*n*   Left-aligns the line at the *n*th column.

JR

Line command JR   **Block command** JJR   Right-aligns the line at the right boundary.

Line command JR*n*   **Block command** JJR*n*   Right-aligns the line at the *n*th column.

KEYDEF

KEYDEF '*key name*'   Displays the definition of a function key.

KEYDEF '*key name*' '*key definition*'   Defines a function key.

Example
KEYDEF 'F9' ':TS'

KEYS

KEYS   Activates the KEYS window.

LEFT

LEFT   LEFT *distance*   Scrolls left.

LIBNAME

LIBNAME   Activates the LIBNAME window. **Alias** LIB

LISTING

LISTING   Activates the OUTPUT window.

LISTING ON *or* OFF   Opens or closes the OUTPUT window. **Release** 6.07+
Alias LIST

LOCK

Equivalent to the LOCK statement. **Release** 6.07+

LOG

LOG   Activates the LOG window.

LOG ON *or* OFF   Opens or closes the LOG window. **Release** 6.07+

M

Line command M*n*   **Block command** MM   Moves lines to the location that is indicated by the A, B, or O line command.

MANAGER

MANAGER   Activates the OUTPUT MANAGER window. **Release** 6.06+

MANAGER ON *or* OFF   Opens or closes the OUTPUT MANAGER window. **Release** 6.07+
Alias MAN, MGR

MARK

MARK MARK CHAR   Marks the beginning or end of a string of text in the active window. The marked text can then be used by the CUT and STORE commands or searched by the FIND and CHANGE commands.

MARK BLOCK   Marks the beginning or end of a rectangular block of text in the active window.

MASK

Line command MASK   Displays a mask line. The mask line is the initial value of inserted lines. **Alias** MA

MEMLIST

MEMLIST *fileref or 'physical PDS name'*   Activates the MEMLIST window. **Operating system** MVS

MZOOM

MZOOM   Displays the message line in a dialog box. Use this command when the message line is longer than the width of the window. **Alias** MZ **Release** 6.07+

NEXT

NEXT NEXT *window*   Activates a different open window.

NOTEPAD

NOTEPAD NOTEPAD *entry*   Activates the NOTEPAD window. **Alias** NOTE

NULLS

NULLS *toggle*   **Mode**   On: trailing blanks in fields are converted to nulls to make inserting text easier. **Operating system** MVS

NUMBERS

NUMBERS *toggle*   **Mode**   On: displays line numbers at the left side of a text editor window. **Alias** NUM, NUMS, NUMBER

O

Line command O   Indicates that text being copied is to be overlaid over this line, or beginning at this line. When text is overlaid, any blanks present in the line are replaced by characters in the text being copied.

OPTIONS

OPTIONS   Activates the OPTIONS window. **Alias** OP, OPT, OPTION

OUTPUT

OUTPUT   Activates the OUTPUT or OUTPUT MANAGER window.

PASTE

PASTE *options*   Copies a paste buffer into the window at the cursor location.

Options

BLOCK Copies text as a block. CHAR Copies text as a string.
BUFFER=*buffer* Uses a named paste buffer.

PCLEAR

PCLEAR   PCLEAR BUFFER=*buffer*   Clears a paste buffer.

PLIST

PLIST   Writes a list of paste buffers in the log.

PMENU

PMENU *toggle*   **Mode**   On: displays menu bars or command lines in
wondows. Off: displays only command lines. **Alias** PM

PREVCMD

PREVCMD   Restores the previously entered command line. **Alias** ?

PREVWIND

PREVWIND   PREVWIND *window*   Activates a different open window.
Alias PREVW

PRINT

PRINT *options*   Prints the contents of the window.

Options APPEND *or* REPLACE FILE=*file* FORM=*form*

PROGRAM

PROGRAM   Activates the PROGRAM EDITOR window.

PROGRAM ON *or* OFF   Opens and closes the PROGRAM EDITOR
window. **Release** 6.07+

Alias PROG, PGM

PRTFILE

PRTFILE   Displays the name of the current print file.

PRTFILE *file options*   Changes the print file. **Options** APPEND A REPLACE R

PRTFILE CLEAR   Closes and dissociates the current print file.

R

Line command R*n*   **Block command** RR*n*   Repeats a line or block a number
of times.

RALIGN

RALIGN *toggle*   **Mode**   On: flowed text is fully justified. Off: flowed text
is left-aligned.

RCHANGE

RCHANGE   Repeats the search and replacement of the most recent
CHANGE command.

RESET

RESET   Cancels all pending line commands and hides special lines.

RESHOW

RESHOW   Redisplays the window.

RESIZE

RESIZE   Returns cascaded or tiled windows to their previous sizes and locations.

RFIND

RFIND   Repeats the most recent text search.

RIGHT

RIGHT   RIGHT *distance*   Scrolls right.

SAVE

SAVE   SAVE *entry options*   Stores the window's data in a catalog entry. **Alias** SAV   **Options** For a window that displays text, the options of the FILE command apply.

SCROLLBAR

SCROLLBAR *toggle*   **Mode**   On: displays scroll bars. **Alias** SBAR

SEQUENCE

SEQUENCE *toggle*   **Mode**   On: removes line numbers from included text. **Alias** SEQ   **Release** 6.07+

SETINIT

SETINIT   Activates the SETINIT window.

SITEINFO

SITEINFO   Activates the SITEINFO window.

SMARK

SMARK   Marks the beginning or end of a rectangular block of text on the screen.

SPELL

SPELL *options*   Checks the spelling of one or more words.

SPELL REMEMBER *or* ADD   SPELL REMEMBER *or* ADD *dictionary*   Adds the last unrecognized word to an auxiliary dictionary.

Options

ALL   Checks every word and lists unrecognized words in a dialog box. NEXT   Finds the next unrecognized word. PREV   Finds the previous unrecognized word.

SUGGEST   ?   If the word is unrecognized, it lists suggestions in a dialog box.

Unrecognized words dialog box commands

ADD REMEMBER ADD *dictionary* REMEMBER *dictionary* Adds the highlighted word to an auxiliary dictionary.

SUGGEST Lists suggestions for the highlighted word.

Suggestions dialog box command

REPLACE Replaces the unrecognized word with the suggestion.

Release 6.06+

STATUS

STATUS *toggle* **Mode** On: displays status information in the upper right corner of active primary windows. **Release** 6.07+

STORE

STORE *options* Copies marked text to a paste buffer.

Options

ALL Copies all marked text. LAST Copies the most recently marked text. This is the default.

APPEND Appends to, rather than replacing, the paste buffer.

BUFFER=*buffer* Uses a named paste buffer.

TABS

Line command TABS Displays a tabs line. Each T in the tabs line represents a tab stop.

Line command TABS*n* Displays a tabs line and sets tab stops every *n* positions.

Alias TAB, TA

TC

Line command TC Connects the line with the following line.

TF

Line command TF Flows text up to the next blank line.

Line command TF*n* Flows text up to the next blank line, using the indicated right margin.

Line command TFA Flows text to the end of the data.

Line command TFA*n* Flows text to the end of the data, using the indicated right margin.

TILE

TILE Tiles all open windows so that they do not overlap.

TITLES

TITLES Activates the TITLES window. **Alias** TITLE

TOP

TOP Scrolls to the top.

TS

Line command TS*n*   Splits the line at the cursor location and inserts lines.

TSO

Equivalent to the TSO statement.

UNDO

Undoes the most recent action in the text editor window, if it was editing or typing.

UNMARK

UNMARK   Unmarks the one marked area that is displayed in the window or the marked area at the cursor location.

UNMARK ALL   Unmarks all marked text in the window. You can then use the FIND and CHANGE commands to search all the text in the window.

UP

UP   UP *distance*   Scrolls up. **Alias for** BACKWARD

VAR

VAR   VAR *SAS dataset*   Activates the VAR window.

VSCROLL

VSCROLL *distance*   Sets the default vertical scrolling distance. **Alias** VS

WDEF

WDEF *top left height width*   Sets the location and size of the window.

WGROW

WGROW   Allows you to increase the size of the window.
Operating system Text

WMOVE

WMOVE   Allows you to move the window. **Operating system** Text

WPOPUP

WPOPUP   Equivalent to the ? selection code for the line at the cursor location. Displays a popup menu. **Release** 6.07+

WSAVE

WSAVE   Saves the location, size, colors, and video attributes of the window in the user profile.

WSAVE ALL   Saves attributes of all open windows.

WSHRINK

WSHRINK   Allows you to decrease the size of the window.
Operating system Text

X
Equivalent to the X statement.

ZOOM
ZOOM *toggle*   **Mode**   On: zooms windows. **Alias** Z

14

Informats

Informats convert text data, such as data from an input text file, to SAS character or numeric values. Informats are most commonly used to read a value for a variable; the type of the informat, character or numeric, must correspond to the type of the variable.

When an informat is specified, the informat name is followed by a period. Depending on the informat, there can be two optional whole number arguments, before and after the period.

In user-entry windows, each field should have a compatible informat and format. Informats marked ✪ in the entries below have a compatible or mostly compatible format with the same name.

Character informats

Character informats use an optional width argument, shown as *w*, which can be between 1 and 200. The default width is usually 1, or the width of a variable or a window field.

$

$*w*. Standard character informat: discards leading blanks; treats period as missing. ✪ **Alias** $F ✪

$ASCII

$ASCII*w*. Reads ASCII text. ✪

$BINARY

$BINARY*w*. Character binary: converts each 8 input binary digit characters to one character. **Release** 6.06+ ✪

$CHAR

$CHAR*w*. Reads text or any data unchanged. ✪

$CHARZB

$CHARZB*w*. Treats nulls (zero bytes) as blanks.

$EBCDIC

$EBCDIC*w*. Reads EBCDIC text. ✪

$HEX

$HEX*w.*   Character hexadecimal: converts each pair of hexadecimal digits to one character. ❂

$OCTAL

$OCTAL*w.*   Character octal: converts each 3 octal digits to one character. **Release** 6.06+ ❂

$PHEX

$PHEX*w.*   *w* ≤ 100   Character packed hexadecimal: converts each input byte to two characters, discarding the last four bits.

$QUOTE

$QUOTE*w.*   Removes leading and trailing quote marks. **Release** 6.07+

$VARYING

$VARYING*w. length variable*   Varying length. Used only in the INPUT statement.

Numeric informats

Numeric informats use optional width and decimal arguments, which are indicated by *w* and *d*. The decimal argument indicates the location of the decimal point, if the input data does not actually contain a period. For binary informats, it indicates that the value is divided by the indicated power of 10 after being read. The default *d* value is 0. Except as noted, the arguments are subject to these restrictions:
$1 \le w \le 32; 0 \le d \le 31$.

Most numeric informats treat fields that contain blanks or a period as standard missing values. Numeric informats that read decimal digits can also treat letters as special missing values if you use the MISSING statement.

Standard numeric informat

w.d   Standard numeric informat: ordinary numeric data and scientific notation. ❂   **Alias** BEST ❂ D, E ❂ F ❂

BINARY

BINARY*w.d*   *w* ≤ 64   Reads binary integers. **Release** 6.06+ ❂

BITS

BITS*w.d*   *d* + *w* ≤ 64   Skips *d* bits, then reads *w* bits as a binary integer. **Release** 6.06+

BZ

BZ*w.d*   Treats blanks as zeros.

COMMA

COMMA*w.d*   Ignores commas, dollar signs, blanks, and parentheses. Treats a leading left parenthesis as a minus sign. ✪   **Alias** DOLLAR ✪

COMMAX

COMMAX*w.d*   The same as COMMA, but with periods and commas interchanged. ✪   **Alias** DOLLARX ✪

FLOAT

FLOAT*w.d* $w = 4$ Single-precision floating point. **Release** 6.07+ ✪

HEX

HEX*w.* $w < 16$ Reads hexadecimal integers. ✪

HEX*w.* $w = 16$ Reads the hexadecimal representation of an 8-byte floating point value. ✪

IB

IB*w.d* $w \le 8, d \le 10$ Signed integer binary. ✪

IEEE

IEEE*w.d* $3 \le w \le 4, d \le 10$ IEEE single-precision floating point. ✪

IEEE*w.d* $5 \le w \le 8, d \le 10$ IEEE double-precision floating point. ✪

Release 6.07+

OCTAL

OCTAL*w.d* $w \le 24$ Reads octal integers. ✪

PD

PD*w.d* $w \le 16, d \le 10$ Packed decimal. ✪

PERCENT

PERCENT*w.*   The same as COMMA, except that if a percent sign follows the value, it is divided by 100. **Release** 6.06+ ✪

PIB

PIB*w.d* $w \le 8, d \le 10$ Unsigned integer binary. ✪

PK

PK*w.d* $w \le 16, d \le 10$ Unsigned packed decimal. ✪

RB

RB*w.d* $2 \le w \le 8, d \le 10$ Real binary; floating point. ✪

S370FIB

S370FIB*w.d* $w \le 8, d \le 10$ IBM System/370 signed integer binary. **Release** 6.06+ ✪

S370FPD

S370FPD*w.d* $w \le 16, d \le 10$ IBM System/370 packed decimal.
Release 6.06+ ✪

S370FPIB

S370FPIB*w.d* $w \le 8, d \le 10$ IBM System/370 unsigned integer binary.
Release 6.06+ ✪

S370FRB

S370FRB*w.d* $2 \le w \le 8, d \le 10$ IBM System/370 real binary.
Release 6.06+ ✪

VAXRB

VAXRB*w.d* $2 \le w \le 8, d \le 10$ VAX real binary. **Release** 6.07+

ZD

ZD*w.d*   Zoned decimal. ✪

ZDB

ZDB*w.*   Zoned decimal with blanks treated as zeros.

ZDV

ZDV*w.d*   Zoned decimal, applied strictly. **Release** 6.07+

Time informats

Time informats are numeric informats that convert text data to SAS date, SAS datetime, and SAS time values.

DATE

DATE*w.* $w \ge 7$ Reads a day, three-letter month abbreviation, and two- or four-digit year as a SAS date value. ✪

DATETIME

DATETIME*w.* $13 \le w \le 40$ Reads a combined DATE and TIME format as a SAS datetime value. ✪

DDMMYY

DDMMYY*w.* $w \ge 6$ Reads a day, month, and year as a SAS date value.
✪

JULIAN

JULIAN*w* $w \ge 5$ Reads a two-digit year and three-digit day of year as a SAS date value. ✪

MINGUO

MINGUO*w* $6 \le w \le 10$ Reads a year, month, and day, with Gregorian 1910 = year 1, as a SAS date value. ✪

MMDDYY

MMDDYY*w.* $w \ge 6$ Reads a month, day, and year as a SAS date value. ✪

MONYY

MONYY*w.* $w \ge 5$ Reads a three-letter month abbreviation and year as a SAS date value. ✪

MSEC

MSEC*w.* $w = 8$ Reads an IBM System/370 time-of-day clock value as a SAS time value.

NENGO

NENGO*w.* $w \ge 7$ Reads a Japanese era (M, T, S, or H), year, month, and day as a SAS date value. ✪

PDTIME

PDTIME*w.* $w = 4$ Reads a packed decimal hour, minute, and second ('0*HHMMSS*F'X) as a SAS time value.

RMFDUR

RMFDUR*w.* $w = 4$ Reads an RMF measurement interval field as a number of seconds.

RMFSTAMP

RMFSTAMP*w.* $w = 8$ Reads an RMF time and date field as a SAS datetime value.

SMFSTAMP

SMFSTAMP*w.* $w = 8$ Reads an SMF time-date field as a SAS datetime value.

TIME

TIME*w.* $w \ge 5$ Reads hours, minutes, and optionally seconds and fractions of seconds as a SAS time value. ✪

TODSTAMP

TODSTAMP*w.* $w = 8$ Reads an IBM System/370 time-of-day clock value as a SAS datetime value.

TU

TU*w.* $w = 4$ Reads an unsigned binary field that contains timer units as a SAS time value. A timer unit is 1/38400 second.

YYMMDD

YYMMDD*w.*   *w* ≥ 6   Reads a year, month, and day as a SAS date value.
✪

YYQ

YYQ*w.*   *w* ≥ 4   Reads a year, the letter Q, and quarter (1–4) as a SAS date value. ✪

15

Formats

A *format* converts a character or numeric value to a text string, as when printing. The use and syntax of formats parallels that of informats. However, the decimal argument is more important for formats than for informats. For most numeric formats, it determines the number of decimal places that are produced.

Character formats

Character formats use an optional width argument, shown as *w*, which can be between 1 and 200.

$

$*w*. Standard character format: discards leading blanks. **Alias** $F

$ASCII

$ASCII*w*. Writes ASCII text.

$BINARY

$BINARY*w*. Character binary: converts each character to 8 output binary digit characters. **Release** 6.06+

$CHAR

$CHAR*w*. Writes a character value unchanged.

$EBCDIC

$EBCDIC*w*. Writes EBCDIC text.

$HEX

$HEX*w*. Character hexadecimal: writes each character as two hexadecimal digits.

$MSGCASE

$MSGCASE*w*. Converts letters to uppercase if the system option MSGCASE is on. **Release** 6.07+

$OCTAL

$OCTAL*w.*   Character octal: writes each character as 3 octal digits.
Release 6.06+

$QUOTE

$QUOTE*w.* $w \geq 3$ Writes string surrounded by double quotes (").
Release 6.07+

$UPCASE

$UPCASE*w.*   Converts lowercase letters to uppercase. **Release** 6.07+

$VARYING

$VARYING*w. length variable*   Varying-length. Used only in the PUT
statement.

Numeric formats

Numeric formats use an optional width argument, *w*, which can range
from 1 to 32. Most also use an optional decimal argument, *d*, which can
range from 0 to 31. For formats that print decimal points, *d* has to be less
than *w*.

Standard numeric format

w.d   Standard numeric format. **Alias** F

BEST

BEST*w.*   Writes a number as precisely as possible in the width.

BINARY

BINARY*w.* $w \leq 64$ Writes binary integers. **Release** 6.06+

COMMA

COMMA*w.d* $w \geq 2$, *d*: 0, 2   Commas separate every three digits.

COMMAX

COMMAX*w.d* $w \geq 2$, *d*: 0, 2   The same as COMMA, but with periods
and commas interchanged.

DOLLAR

DOLLAR*w.d* $w \geq 2$, *d*: 0, 2   The same as COMMA, but preceded by a
dollar sign.

DOLLARX

DOLLARX*w.d* $w \geq 2$, *d*: 0, 2   The same as DOLLAR, but with periods and
commas interchanged.

E

E*w*.   *w* ≥ 7   Scientific (exponential) notation using E.

FLOAT

FLOAT*w.d*   *w* = 4   Single-precision floating point. **Release** 6.07+

FRACT

FRACT*w*.   *w* ≥ 4   Writes fractions in reduced form. **Release** 6.06+

HEX

HEX*w*.   *w* < 16   Writes hexadecimal integers.

HEX*w*.   *w* = 16   Writes the hexadecimal representation of an 8-byte floating point value.

IB

IB*w.d*   *w* ≤ 8, *d* ≤ 10   Signed integer binary.

IEEE

IEEE*w.d*   3 ≤ *w* ≤ 4   IEEE single-precision floating point.

IEEE*w.d*   5 ≤ *w* ≤ 8   IEEE double-precision floating point.

Release 6.07+

NEGPAREN

NEGPAREN*w.d*   *d*: 0, 2   Commas separate every three digits; negative numbers are in parentheses. **Release** 6.06+

OCTAL

OCTAL*w*.   *w* ≤ 24   Writes octal integers.   **Release** 6.06+

PD

PD*w.d*   *w* ≤ 16, *d* ≤ 10   Packed decimal.

PERCENT

PERCENT*w.d*   *w* ≥ 3   Writes numbers as percents, followed by a percent sign, with negative values enclosed in parentheses. **Release** 6.06+

PIB

PIB*w.d*   *w* ≤ 8, *d* ≤ 10   Unsigned integer binary.

PK

PK*w.d*   *w* ≤ 16, *d* ≤ 10   Unsigned packed decimal.

RB

RB*w.d*   2 ≤ *w* ≤ 8, *d* ≤ 10   Real binary; floating point.

ROMAN

ROMANw. $w \geq 2$ Writes Roman numerals using capital letters.

S370FIB

S370FIBw.d $w \leq 8, d \leq 10$ IBM System/370 signed integer binary.
Release 6.06+

S370FPD

S370FPDw.d $w \leq 16, d \leq 10$ IBM System/370 packed decimal.
Release 6.06+

S370FPIB

S370FPIBw.d $w \leq 8, d \leq 10$ IBM System/370 unsigned integer binary.
Release 6.06+

S370FRB

S370FRBw.d $2 \leq w \leq 8, d \leq 10$ IBM System/370 real binary.
Release 6.06+

SSN

SSNw. $w = 11$ Nine-digit number with hyphens after the third and
fifth digits.

WORDF

WORDFw. $5 \leq w \leq 200$ Writes number in words, with hundredths
written as a fraction.

WORDS

WORDSw. $5 \leq w \leq 200$ Writes number in words, with hundredths
written in words.

Z

Zw.d   Writes number with leading zeros.

ZD

ZDw.d   Zoned decimal.

Time formats

Time formats are formats that write SAS date, SAS time, and SAS datetime
values. Widths up to 32 are often allowed, but the useful widths are
shown in the entries. Instead of descriptions, examples are shown of the
output that is produced by each format.

DATE

DATEw. w: 5, 7, 9   Writes a SAS date value: 06SEP93 06SEP1993

DATETIME

DATETIME*w.d*   *w*: 7, 10, 13, 16, 18–40; *d* ≤ 39; *d* = *w* – 18   Writes a SAS datetime value: 06SEP93 06SEP93:14 06SEP93:14:03 06SEP93:14:03:17 06SEP1993:14:03:17.83

DAY

DAY*w.*   *w* = 2   Writes the day of the month of a SAS date value. **Release 6.06+**

DDMMYY

DAY*w.*   *w*: 2, 4, 5, 6, 8   Writes a SAS date value: 06 0609 06/09 060993 06/09/93 **Release 6.06+**

DOWNAME

DOWNAME*w.*   *w*: 1, 2, 3, 9   Writes the name of the day of the week of a SAS date value. **Release 6.06+**

HHMM

HHMM*w.d*   *w*: 2, 4–20, *d* = *w* – 6   Writes a SAS time value: 15 1547 15:47

HOUR

HOUR*w.d*   2 ≤*w* ≤ 20, *d* < *w* – 2   Writes the hour of a SAS time value.

JULDAY

JULDAY*w.*   *w* = 3   Writes the day of the year of a SAS date value. **Release 6.06+**

JULIAN

JULIAN*w.*   *w* = 5, 7   Writes the year and day of the year of a SAS date value.

MINGUO

MINGUO*w.*   *w* : 6–7, 8–10   Writes a SAS date value with Gregorian 1910 = year 1: 840922 0084/09/22 **Release 6.07+**

MMDDYY

MMDDYY*w.*   *w* = 2, 4, 5, 6, 8   Writes a SAS date value: 09 0922 09/22 092293 09/22/93

MMSS

MMSS*w.d*   *w*: 2, 5, 7–20, *d* = *w* – 6   Writes a SAS time value or a number of seconds as minutes and seconds, or writes a number of minutes as hours and minutes: 24:10

MMYY

MMYY*w*.   *w* = 5, 7   Writes the month and year of a SAS date value:
09M93 09M1993 **Release 6.06+**

MMYYC

MMYYC*w*.   *w* = 5, 7   Writes the month and year of a SAS date value:
09:93 09:1993 **Release 6.06+**

MMYYD

MMYYD*w*.   *w* = 5, 7   Writes the month and year of a SAS date value:
09-93 09-1993 **Release 6.06+**

MMYYN

MMYYN*w*.   *w* = 4, 6   Writes the month and year of a SAS date value:
0993 091993 **Release 6.06+**

MMYYP

MMYYP*w*.   *w* = 5, 7   Writes the month and year of a SAS date value:
09.93 09.1993 **Release 6.06+**

MMYYS

MMYYS*w*.   *w* = 5, 7   Writes the month and year of a SAS date value:
09/93 09/1993 **Release 6.06+**

MONNAME

MONNAME*w*.   *w*: 1, 3, 9   Writes the name of the month of a SAS date
value: September **Release 6.06+**

MONTH

MONTH*w*.   *w* = 2   Writes the month number of a SAS date value.
Release 6.06+

MONYY

MONYY*w*.   *w* = 5, 7   Writes the month and year of a SAS date value:
APR11 APR2011

NENGO

NENGO*w*. $2 \le w \le 10$ Writes the Japanese era (M, T, S, or H), year,
month, and day of a SAS date value. **Release 6.06+**

QTR

QTR*w*.   *w* = 1   Writes the quarter number of a SAS date value.
Release 6.06+

QTRR

QTRR*w*.   *w* = 3   Writes the quarter number of a SAS date value as a
Roman numeral. **Release 6.06+**

TIME

TIME*w.*   *w* = 2, 5, 8, 10–11, *d* = *w* – 9   Writes a SAS time value as hours and optional minutes, seconds, and fractional seconds: 05   05:15   05:15:00 05:15:00.00

TOD

TOD*w.*   *w* = 2, 5, 8   Writes the time of day of a SAS datetime value or a SAS time value as hours and optional minutes, seconds, and fractional seconds.

WEEKDATE

WEEKDATE*w.*   *w* = 3, 9, 15, 17, 23, 29   Writes a SAS date value: Mon Monday Mon, Oct 12, 92 Mon, Oct 12, 1992 Monday, Oct 12, 1992 Monday, October 12, 1992

WEEKDATX

WEEKDATX*w.*   *w* = 3, 9, 15, 17, 23, 29   Writes a SAS date value: Mon Monday Mon, 12 Oct 92 Monday, 12 October 1992

WEEKDAY

WEEKDAY*w.*   *w* = 1   Writes the number of the day of the week of a SAS date value, with Sunday=1, Saturday=7. **Release 6.06+**

WORDDATE

WORDDATE*w.*   *w* = 3, 6, 9, 12, 18   Writes a SAS date value: Oct Oct 12 October Oct 12, 92 Oct 12, 1992

WORDDATX

WORDDATE*w.*   *w* = 3, 6, 9, 12, 18   Writes a SAS date value: Oct 12 Oct 12 Oct 92 12 Oct 1992

YEAR

YEAR*w.*   *w* = 2, 4   Writes the year of a SAS date value: 92 1992 **Release 6.06+**

YYMM

YYMM*w.*   *w* = 5, 7   Writes the year and month of a SAS date value: 93M09 1993M09 **Release 6.06+**

YYMMC

YYMMC*w.*   *w* = 5, 7   Writes the year and month of a SAS date value: 93:09 1993:09 **Release 6.06+**

YYMMD

YYMMD*w.*   *w* = 5, 7   Writes the year and month of a SAS date value: 93-09 1993-09 **Release 6.06+**

YYMMDD

YYMMDDw.   *w* = 2, 4, 5, 6, 8   Writes the year, month, and day of a SAS date value: 93 9309 93/09 930922 93/09/22

YYMMN

YYMMNw.   *w* = 4, 6   Writes the year and month of a SAS date value: 9309 199309 **Release** 6.06+

YYMMP

YYMMPw.   *w* = 5, 7   Writes the year and month of a SAS date value: 93.09 1993.09 **Release** 6.06+

YYMMS

YYMMw.   *w* = 5, 7   Writes the year and month of a SAS date value: 93/09 1993/09 **Release** 6.06+

YYMON

YYMONw.   *w* = 5, 7   Writes the year and month of a SAS date value: 93SEP 1993SEP **Release** 6.06+

YYQ

YYQw.   *w* = 4, 6   Writes the year and quarter of a SAS date value: 00Q4 2000Q4

YYQC

YYQCw.   *w* = 4, 6   Writes the year and quarter of a SAS date value: 00:4 2000:4 **Release** 6.06+

YYQD

YYQDw.   *w* = 4, 6   Writes the year and quarter of a SAS date value: 00-4 2000-4 **Release** 6.06+

YYQN

YYQNw.   *w* = 3, 5   Writes the year and quarter of a SAS date value: 004 20004 **Release** 6.06+

YYQP

YYQPw.   *w* = 4, 6   Writes the year and quarter of a SAS date value: 00.4 2000.4 **Release** 6.06+

YYQR

YYQRw.   *w* = 6, 8   Writes the year and quarter of a SAS date value: 00QIV 2000QIV **Release** 6.06+

YYQRC

YYQRCw.   *w* = 6, 8   Writes the year and quarter of a SAS date value: 00:IV 2000:IV **Release** 6.06+

YYQRD

YYQRD*w.*   *w* = 6, 8   Writes the year and quarter of a SAS date value:
00–IV   2000–IV   **Release** 6.06+

YYQRN

YYQRN*w.*   *w* = 5, 7   Writes the year and quarter of a SAS date value:
00IV   2000IV   **Release** 6.06+

YYQRP

YYQRP*w.*   *w* = 6, 8   Writes the year and quarter of a SAS date value:
00.IV   2000.IV   **Release** 6.06+

YYQRS

YYQRS*w.*   *w* = 6, 8   Writes the year and quarter of a SAS date value:
00/IV   2000/IV   **Release** 6.06+

YYQS

YYQS*w.*   *w* = 4, 6   Writes the year and quarter of a SAS date value:
00/4   2000/4   **Release** 6.06+

16
Functions

Functions are used in data step programming. A function call can be used as an expression or as part of an expression.

Function types

A function returns either character or numeric values and is classed as a character function or a numeric function. The INPUT function is an exception that can return either a character value or a numeric value, depending on its arguments.

Lengths of character functions

The length of the value returned by a character function is measured in two ways. The *expression length* — the length of the value if it is used in an expression — usually depends on the values of the function's arguments. The *memory length* — the amount of memory used to hold the returned value — usually depends on the memory length of one of the arguments. Memory lengths of some functions might change in later releases.

Function arguments

A *function call* consists of the function name followed by a list of arguments in parentheses:

> function(argument, argument, . . .)

Arguments are expressions whose values are used by the function. Each argument should be of a particular type. Most numeric functions use only numeric arguments. Character arguments are also common. A few functions use other types of arguments.

The numeric arguments of many functions are limited to a particular range of values. If a numeric value outside that range is used as an argument, the function returns a missing value or generates an error condition.

OF

When you use several variables as arguments to a function, you can list arguments in an alternate way. Instead of separating the arguments by commas, you can use the keyword OF and a variable list. In a variable list, variable names are separated by blanks:

```
function(OF variable variable ...)
```

You can use abbreviated variable lists; they are especially useful for statistic functions.

Function reference

Each entry shows the function's type, length (for character functions), and syntax and describes the use of the function.

These symbols are used for arguments:

x	number
n	whole number
θ	angle measurement in radians
X	random variate, in the range of a probability distribution
P	probability, between 0 and 1
string	character value that represents a string
char	single character
chars	character value that represents a set of characters
code	character code that is defined by the function
sample	a set of numbers for statistical analysis

Numeric functions are identified by the symbol **N**. For character functions, the symbol **$** is followed by the memory length and expression length of the function. The memory length is always greater than or equal to the expression length.

ABS
ABS(x)   **N**   Returns the absolute value.

AIRY
AIRY(x)   **N**   The airy function. **Release** 6.07+

ARCOS
ARCOS(x)   **N**   *Trig.* Returns the arc cosine. The inverse of the cosine function.

ARSIN
ARSIN(x)   **N**   *Trig.* Returns the arc sine. The inverse of the sine function.

ATAN
ATAN(x)   **N**   *Trig.* Returns the arc tangent. The inverse of the tangent function.

BAND
BAND(n, n) $0 \leq n < 2^{32}$ **N**   *Bitwise.* Returns the bitwise logical AND operation on the two whole numbers. **Release** 6.07+

BETAINV

BETAINV(P, α, β)   **N**   *Probability.* The inverse distribution function of the beta distribution with the parameters α and β.

BLSHIFT

BLSHIFT(n, *distance*) $0 \leq n < 2^{32}$, $0 \leq distance \leq 31$ **N**   *Bitwise.* Returns the whole number shifted left by the indicated distance. **Release** 6.07+

Example BLSHIFT(15, 3) is 120.

BNOT

BNOT(n) $0 \leq n < 2^{32}$ **N**   *Bitwise.* Returns the bitwise logical NOT operation on the whole number. **Release** 6.07+

BOR

BOR(n, n) $0 \leq n < 2^{32}$ **N**   *Bitwise.* Returns the bitwise logical OR operation on the two whole numbers. **Release** 6.07+

BRSHIFT

BRSHIFT(n, *distance*) $0 \leq n < 2^{32}$, $0 \leq distance \leq 31$ **N**   *Bitwise.* Returns the whole number shifted right by the indicated distance. **Release** 6.07+

Example BRSHIFT(15, 3) is 1.

BXOR

BXOR(n, n) $0 \leq n < 2^{32}$ **N**   *Bitwise.* Returns the bitwise logical exclusive OR operation on the two whole numbers. **Release** 6.07+

BYTE

BYTE(n)   **$** 1/1   Returns a character from the standard character set (ASCII or EBCDIC, depending on the computer).

CEIL

CEIL(x)   **N**   *Rounding.* Returns the smallest integer greater than or equal to the argument.

CINV

CINV(P, *d.f.*)   CINV(P, *d.f.*, *noncentrality*)   **N**   *Probability.* The inverse distribution function of the chi-squared distribution with the indicated parameters. **Release** 6.06+

CNONCT

CNONCT(x, *d.f.*, P)   **N**   *Probability.* Returns the nonnegative noncentrality parameter for a noncentral chi-square distribution with the indicated parameters. **Release** 6.07+

COLLATE

COLLATE($n1$, $n2$)   COLLATE($n1$, , *length*)   COLLATE($n1$)   **$** 200/varies
Returns a segment of the standard character set (ASCII or EBCDIC, depending on the computer). The segment begins with character number $n1$ and includes consecutive characters that continue to character number

n2, to the indicated length, or to the end of the character set (up to a maximum length of 200).

COMPBL

COMPBL(*string*)   **$** string's memory length/varies   Returns the string with any consecutive blanks converted to single blanks. **Release** 6.07+

COMPOUND

COMPOUND(*a, f, r, n*)   **N**   *Financial.* Compound interest is described by an initial amount (*a*), a final amount (*f*), an interest rate (*r*), and a length of time (*n*). Provide any three of these values, and the function calculates the remaining value.

Example COMPOUND(1, 2, .07, .) calculates how long it takes for money to double at 7% interest.

COMPRESS

COMPRESS(*string, chars*)   COMPRESS(*string*)   **$** string's memory length/varies   Returns the string with the indicated characters (or blanks) removed.

COS

COS(*θ*)   **N**   *Trig.* Returns the cosine of the angle.

Example COS(3.14159) is −1.

COSH

COSH(*θ*)   **N**   *Trig.* Returns the hyperbolic cosine of the angle.

CSS

CSS(*sample*)   **N**   *Statistic.* The corrected sum of squares.

CV

CV(*sample*)   **N**   *Statistic.* The coefficient of variation.

DACCDB

DACCDB(*age, value, recovery period, rate*)   **N**   *Depreciation.* How much the value of an asset has depreciated, using the declining balance method.

DACCDBSL

DACCDBSL(*age, value, recovery period, rate*)   **N**   *Depreciation.* How much the value of an asset has depreciated, using the declining balance method switching to the straight-line method.

DACCSL

DACCSL(*age, value, recovery period*)   **N**   *Depreciation.* How much the value of an asset has depreciated, using the straight-line method.

DACCSYD

DACCSL(*age, value, recovery period*)   **N**   *Depreciation.* How much the value of an asset has depreciated, using the sum-of-years-digits method.

DACCTAB

DACCTAB(*age, value, rate1, rate2, . . .*)   **N**   *Depreciation.* How much the value of an asset has depreciated, using the rates provided.

DAIRY

DAIRY(x)   **N**   The derivative of the airy function. **Release** 6.07+

DATE

DATE()   **N**   Returns the current date.

DATEJUL

DATEJUL(*SAS date*)   **N**   Returns "Julian" date number.

DATEPART

DATEPART(*SAS datetime*)   **N**   Returns SAS date.

DATETIME

DATETIME()   **N**   Returns the current date and time.

DAY

DAY(*SAS date*)   **N**   Returns day of month.

DEPDB

DEPDB(*age, value, recovery period, rate*)   **N**   *Depreciation.* How much the value of an asset depreciates in a year, ending at the indicated age, using the declining balance method.

DEPDBSL

DEPDBSL(*age, value, recovery period, rate*)   **N**   *Depreciation.* How much the value of an asset depreciates in a year, ending at the indicated age, using the declining balance method switching to the straight-line method.

DEPSL

DEPSL(*age, value, recovery period*)   **N**   *Depreciation.* How much the value of an asset depreciates in a year, ending at the indicated age, using the straight-line method.

DEPSYD

DEPSL(*age, value, recovery period*)   **N**   *Depreciation.* How much the value of an asset depreciates in a year, ending at the indicated age, using the sum-of-years-digits method.

DEPTAB

DEPTAB(*age, value, rate1, rate2, . . .*)   **N**   *Depreciation.* How much the value of an asset depreciates in a year, ending at the indicated age, using the rates provided.

DEQUOTE

DEQUOTE(*string*)   **$** string's memory length/varies   Returns the string with quotes removed and quoted quotes reduced. **Release** 6.07+

Example DEQUOTE("'Don''t'") is "Don't".

DHMS

DHMS(*SAS date, hour, minute, second*)   **N**   Returns SAS datetime.

DIF

DIF(*value*)   DIF*n*(*value*)   **N**   Returns the result of subtracting from the argument the value supplied in the *n*th previous execution of the function call. Returns a standard missing value the first *n* times.

DIGAMMA

DIGAMMA(*x*)   **N**   The derivative of the log gamma function.

DIM

DIM(*array*)   **N**   Returns the size of a one-dimensional explicitly subscripted array.

DIM(*array, n*)   DIM*n*(*array*)   **N**   Returns the size of dimension *n* of an explicitly subscripted array.

ERF

ERF(*x*)   **N**   The error function.

ERFC

ERFC(*x*)   **N**   Returns 1 – ERF(X).

EXP

EXP(*x*)   **N**   Exponential function: returns e^x.

FINV

FINV(*P, n.d.f., d.d.f., noncentrality*)   **N**   *Probability.* The inverse distribution function of the *F* distribution with the indicated parameters. **Release** 6.06+

FIPNAME

FIPNAME(*FIPS state number*)   **$** 200/varies   Returns the state name in uppercase letters.

FIPNAMEL

FIPNAMEL(*FIPS state number*)   **$** 200/varies   Returns the state name.

FIPSTATE

FIPSTATE(*FIPS state number*)   **$** 200/2   Returns the 2-letter postal code for the state.

FLOOR

FLOOR(*x*)   **N**   *Rounding*. Returns the smallest integer that is less than or equal to the argument.

Example FLOOR(101.25) is 101.

FNONCT

FNONCT(*x, n.d.f., d.d.f., P*)   **N**   *Probability*. Returns the nonnegative noncentrality parameter for a noncentral F distribution with the indicated parameters. **Release** 6.07+

FUZZ

FUZZ(*x*)   **N**   *Rounding*. Returns the integer if the argument is within 10^{-12} of an integer; otherwise, it returns the argument.

GAMINV

GAMINV(*P, a*)   **N**   *Probability*. The inverse distribution function of the gamma distribution with the indicated *a* parameter and *b* = 1.

GAMMA

GAMMA(*x*)   **N**   The gamma function: $\Gamma(x)$.

HBOUND

HBOUND(*array*)   **N**   Returns the upper bound of a one-dimensional explicitly subscripted array.

HBOUND(*array, n*)   HBOUND*n*(*array*)   **N**   Returns the upper bound of dimension *n* of an explicitly subscripted array.

HMS

HMS(*hour, minute, second*)   **N**   Returns SAS time value, or a duration of time in seconds.

HOUR

HOUR(*SAS time or SAS datetime*)   **N**   Returns the hour of the day.

IBESSEL

IBESSEL(*v, x, kode*)   **N**   Returns the modified bessel function of *x*. **Release** 6.07+

INDEX

INDEX(*string, substring*)   **N**   Returns the first location of the substring in the string.

INDEXC

INDEXC(*string, chars*)   **N**   Returns the first location of any of the characters in the string.

INDEXW

INDEXW(*string, substring*)   **N**   Returns the first location of the substring as a word or at the beginning of a word in the string. **Release** 6.07+

INPUT

INPUT(*text, optional error control character informat specification*) **$**
informat width   Applies the informat specification to the text.

INPUT(*text, optional error control numeric informat specification*)   **N**
Applies the informat specification to the text.

Error controls For invalid data: ? Suppresses log messages.
?? Also prevents _ERROR_ from being set to 1. **Release 6.06+**

Example INPUT('444', 3.2) is 4.44.

INPUTC

INPUTC(*text, character informat specification value, optional width
specification*)   **$** 200/informat width   Applies the informat specification
to the text. **Release 6.07+**

INPUTN

INPUTN(*text, numeric informat specification value, optional width
specification, optional decimal specification*)   **N**   Applies the informat
specification to the text. **Release 6.07+**

Example INPUTN('444', '3.2') is 4.44.

INT

INT(*x*)   **N**   *Rounding.* Removes the fractional part of the number,
returning the integer part.

INTCK

INTCK(*interval code, SAS date, SAS date*)   *interval code*: 'DAY', 'WEEK',
'MONTH', 'QTR', 'YEAR'   **N**   Returns the number of intervals from the first
SAS date to the second SAS date.

INTCK(*interval code, SAS datetime, SAS datetime*)   *interval code*: 'SECOND',
'MINUTE', 'HOUR', 'DAY', 'DTDAY', 'DTWEEK', 'DTMONTH', 'DTQTR', 'DTYEAR'
N   Returns the number of intervals from the first SAS datetime to the
second SAS datetime.

INTCK(*interval code, SAS time, SAS time*)   *interval code*: 'SECOND', 'MINUTE',
'HOUR'   **N**   Returns the number of intervals from the first SAS time to the
second SAS time.

INTNX

INTNX(*interval code, SAS date, n*)   *interval code*: 'DAY', 'WEEK', 'MONTH',
'QTR', 'YEAR'   **N**   Returns the SAS date advanced by the indicated
number of intervals.

INTNX(*interval code, SAS datetime, n*)   *interval code*: 'SECOND', 'MINUTE',
'HOUR', 'DAY', 'DTDAY', 'DTWEEK', 'DTMONTH', 'DTQTR', 'DTYEAR'   **N**
Returns the SAS datetime advanced by the indicated number of intervals.

INTNX(*interval code, SAS time, n*)   *interval code*: 'SECOND', 'MINUTE', 'HOUR'
N   Returns the SAS time advanced by the indicated number of intervals.

INTRR

INTRR(*number of payment periods per year, amount 1, amount 2, ...*)   **N**
Returns the internal rate of return.

IRR

IRR(*number of payment periods per year, amount 1, amount 2, . . .*)   **N**
Returns the internal rate of return as a percent.

JBESSEL

JBESSEL(*v, x*)   **N**   Returns the bessel function of *x*. **Release** 6.07+

JULDATE

JULDATE(*"Julian" date number*)   **N**   Returns the SAS date.

KURTOSIS

KURTOSIS(*sample*)   **N**   *Statistic.* The kurtosis.

LAG

LAG(*numeric value*)   LAG*n*(*numeric value*)   **N**   Returns the value that
was supplied in the *n*th previous execution of the function call. Returns a
standard missing value the first *n* times.

LAG(*character value*)   LAG*n*(*character value*)   **$ 200/varies**   Returns
the value that was supplied in the *n*th previous execution of the function
call. Returns a blank value the first *n* times.

LBOUND

LBOUND(*array*)   **N**   Returns the lower bound of a one-dimensional
explicitly subscripted array.

LBOUND(*array, n*)   LBOUND*n*(*array*)   **N**   Returns the lower bound of
dimension *n* of an explicitly subscripted array.

LEFT

LEFT(*string*)   **$ string's memory length/string's length**   Left-aligns:
converts leading blanks to trailing blanks.

LENGTH

LENGTH(*string*)   **N**   Returns the length of the string, not counting
trailing blanks. For a null string, returns 1.

LGAMMA

LGAMMA(*x*)   **N**   The log gamma function. Returns LOG(GAMMA(X)).

LOG

LOG(*x*)   **N**   The natural logarithm function. Returns the base *e*
logarithm of the number.

LOG2

LOG2(*x*)   **N**   Returns the base 2 logarithm of the number.

LOG10

LOG10(*x*)   **N**   Returns the base 10 (common) logarithm of the number.
Example   LOG10(1000) is 3.

LOWCASE

LOWCASE(*string*)   **$** string's memory length/string's length   Converts uppercase letters to lowercase. **Release** 6.07+

MAX

MAX(*sample*)   **N**   *Statistic.* The maximum.

MDY

MDY(*month, day, year*)   **N**   Returns the SAS date.

MEAN

MEAN(*sample*)   **N**   *Statistic.* The mean; average.

MIN

MIN(*sample*)   **N**   *Statistic.* The minimum.

MINUTE

MINUTE(*SAS time or SAS datetime*)   **N**   Returns the minute.

MOD

MOD(*x, modulus*)   **N**   Returns the remainder that results from dividing *x* by *modulus*.

MONTH

MONTH(*SAS date*)   **N**   Returns the month.

MORT

MORT(*a, p, r, n*)   **N**   *Financial.* A simple loan can described by an amount (*a*), a payment amount (*p*), a periodic interest rate (*r*), and a length of time (*n*). Provide any three of these values and the function calculates the remaining value.

N

N(*sample*)   **N**   *Statistic.* The number of nonmissing arguments.

NETPV

NETPV(*interest rate, number of payment periods per year, amount 1, amount 2, . . .*)   **N**   Returns the net present value.

NMISS

NMISS(*sample*)   **N**   *Statistic.* The number of missing arguments.

NORMAL

NORMAL(*seed*);   Returns a random number from a normal distribution with $\mu = 0$ and $\sigma = 1$.

NPV

NPV(*interest rate as a percent, number of payment periods per year, amount 1, amount 2, . . .*)   **N**   Returns the net present value.

ORDINAL

ORDINAL(*n, sample*);   Returns the *n*th lowest value in the sample.

POISSON

POISSON(λ, *X*);   *Probability.* The Poisson distribution function.

PROBBETA

PROBBETA(α, β);   *Probability.* The beta distribution function.

PROBBNML

PROBBNML(*P, n, X*);   *Probability.* The binomial distribution function.

PROBCHI

PROBCHI(*X, d.f., noncentrality*);   *Probability.* The chi-squared distribution function.

PROBF

PROBF(*X, n.d.f., d.d.f., noncentrality*);   *Probability.* The *F* distribution function.

PROBGAM

PROBGAM(*X, a*);   The gamma distribution function with *b* = 1.

PROBHYPR

PROBHYPR(*nn, k, n, X, odds ratio*);   The hypergeometric distribution function.

PROBIT

PROBIT(*P*)   **N**   *Probability.* The inverse distribution function of the normal distribution with μ = 0 and σ = 1.

PROBNEGB

PROBNEGB(*P, n, X*);   *Probability.* The negative binomial distribution function.

PROBNORM

PROBNORM(*X*);   *Probability.* The normal distribution function with μ = 0 and σ = 1.

PROBT

PROBT(*X, d.f., noncentrality*);   *Probability.* The *t* distribution function.

PUT

PUT(*character value, character format specification*)   PUT(*numeric value, numeric format specification*)   **$** format width   Applies the format specification to the value.

Example PUT(4, Z5.) is '00004'.

PUTC

PUTC(*character value, character format specification value, optional width specification*)   **$** 200/varies   Applies the format specification to the value. **Release** 6.07+

PUTN

PUTN(*numeric value, numeric format specification value, optional width specification, optional decimal specification*)   **$** 200/varies   Applies the format specification to the value. **Release** 6.07+

Example   PUT(4, 'Z5.') is '00004'.

QTR

QTR(*SAS date*)   **N**   Returns the quarter.

QUOTE

QUOTE(*string*)   **$** 200/varies   Produces a quoted string from the argument: encloses it in double quotes and doubles any double quotes it contains. **Release** 6.07+

RANBIN

RANBIN(*seed, n, P*);   Returns a random number from a binomial distribution.

RANCAU

RANCAU(*seed*);   Returns a random number from a Cauchy distribution with $\alpha = 1$ and $\beta = 1$.

RANEXP

RANEXP(*seed*);   Returns a random number from an exponential distribution with $\lambda = 1$.

RANGAM

RANGAM(*seed, a*);   Returns a random number from a gamma distribution with $b = 1$. **Release** 6.06+

RANGE

RANGE(*sample*)   **N**   *Statistic.* The range.

RANK

RANK(*char*)   **$** 1/1   Returns the character's number in the standard character set.

RANNOR

RANNOR(*seed*);   Returns a random number from a normal distribution with $\mu = 0$ and $\sigma = 1$.

RANPOI

RANPOI(*seed, λ*);   Returns a random number from a Poisson distribution.

RANTBL

RANTBL(*seed, f(1), f(2), . . .*);   Returns a random counting number from the indicated distribution.

RANTRI

RANTRI(*seed, hypotenuse*);   Returns a random number from a triangular distribution on the interval [0, 1].

RANUNI

RANUNI(*seed*);   Returns a random number from the uniform distribution on the interval [0, 1].

REPEAT

REPEAT(*string, n*)   **$** 200/varies   Returns the string repeated $n + 1$ times.

RESOLVE

RESOLVE(*text*)   **$** 200/varies   Resolves the macro expression that is contained in the character argument and returns the resolved macro expression. **Release** 6.07+

REVERSE

REVERSE(*string*)   **$** string's memory length/string's length   Reverses the order of characters in the string.

Example REVERSE('forward') is 'drawrof'.

RIGHT

RIGHT(*string*)   **$** string's memory length/string's length   Right-aligns: converts trailing blanks to leading blanks.

ROUND

ROUND(*n*)   **N**   Rounds n to the nearest integer.

ROUND(*n, unit*)   **N**   Rounds n to the nearest multiple of *unit*.

Example ROUND(17, 3) is 18.

SAVING

SAVING(*f, p, r, n*)   **N**   *Financial.* A series of payments can be described by a final value (*f*), a payment amount (*p*), a periodic interest rate (*r*), and a length of time (*n*). Provide any three of these values, and the function calculates the remaining value.

SCAN

SCAN(*string, n, delimiters*)   **$** 200/varies   Returns the *n*th token from the string.

SECOND

SECOND(*SAS time or SAS datetime*)   **N**   Returns the second.

SIGN

SIGN(*x*)   **N**   Returns –1 if *x* is negative, 0 if *x* is 0, 1 if *x* is positive.

SIN

SIN(*θ*)   **N**   *Trig.* Returns the sine of the angle.

SINH

SIN(*θ*)   **N**   *Trig.* Returns the hyperbolic sine of the angle.

SKEWNESS

SKEWNESS(*sample*)   **N**   *Statistic.* The skewness.

SLEEP

SLEEP(*n*)   **N**   Suspends execution and displays a dialog box for *n* seconds. Returns the number of seconds execution was suspended. **Operating system** OS/2

SOUNDEX

SOUNDEX(*word*)   **$** string's memory length/varies   Encodes a word according to the Soundex algorithm: discards some letters and converts consonants to digits. **Release 6.07+**

Example SOUNDEX('cardboard') is 'C63163'.

SQRT

SQRT(*x*)   **N**   Returns the square root.

STD

STD(*sample*)   **N**   *Statistic.* The standard deviation.

STDERR

STDERR(*sample*)   **N**   *Statistic.* The standard error of the mean.

STFIPS

STFIPS(*2–letter postal code for state*)   **N**   Returns the FIPS state number.

STNAME

STNAME(*2–letter postal code for state*)   **$** 200/varies   Returns the state name in uppercase letters.

STNAMEL

STNAMEL(*2–letter postal code for state*)   **$** 200/varies   Returns the state name.

SUBSTR

SUBSTR(*string, start*)   SUBSTR(*string, start, length*)   **$** string's memory length/varies   Returns the substring.

SUM

SUM(*sample*)   **N**   *Statistic.* The sum.

SYMGET

SYMGET(*macrovariable name*) **$** 200/varies   Returns the value of the macrovariable.

SYSPROD

SYSPROD(*name*) **N** *name*: AF, ASSIST, ETS, FSP, GRAPH, etc.   Returns SAS product licensing information: 1 if the name is a licensed SAS product, 0 if the name is an unlicensed SAS product, –1 if the name is not a SAS product. A 1 value suggests, but does not ensure, that the product is installed and available for use. **Release** 6.07+

Example SYSPROD('BASE') is 1.

TAN

TAN(θ) **N** *Trig.* Returns the tangent of the angle.

TANH

TANH(θ) **N** *Trig.* Returns the hyperbolic tangent of the angle.

TIME

TIME() **N**   Returns the current time of day.

TIMEPART

TIMEPART(*SAS datetime*) **N**   Returns the SAS time.

TINV

TINV(*P, d.f., noncentrality*) **N** *Probability.* The inverse distribution function of the *t* distribution with the indicated parameters. **Release** 6.06+

TNONCT

TNONCT(*x, d.f., P*) **N** *Probability.* Returns the nonnegative noncentrality parameter for a noncentral *t* distribution with the parameters indicated. **Release** 6.07+

TODAY

TODAY() **N**   Returns the current date.

TRANSLATE

TRANSLATE(*string, replacement chars, chars, . . .*) **$** string's memory length/string's length   Returns the string with all occurrences of the characters replaced by the corresponding replacement characters.

TRANWRD

TRANWRD(*string, substring, replacement substring*) **$** 200/varies Returns the string with all occurrences of the substring replaced by the replacement substring. **Release** 6.07+

TRIGAMMA

TRIGAMMA(*x*) **N**   The second derivative of the log gamma function.

TRIM

TRIM(*string*) $ string's memory length/varies   Returns the string with trailing blanks removed. For a blank argument, it returns a single blank.

TRIMN

TRIMN(*string*) $ string's memory length/varies   Returns the string with trailing blanks removed. For a blank argument, it returns a null string. **Release** 6.07+

TRUNC

TRUNC(*x, length*)   **N**   Shortens the number to the indicated length in bytes, which reduces its precision. **Release** 6.06+

Example TRUNC(844.5001, 3) is 844.5.

TSO

TSO(*command*)   **N**   Executes the TSO command. Returns an error code. **Operating system** MVS   **Mode** Foreground

UNIFORM

UNIFORM(*seed*);   Returns a random number from the uniform distribution on the interval [0, 1].

UPCASE

UPCASE(*string*) $ string's memory length/string's length   Converts lowercase letters to uppercase. **Release** 6.07+

USS

USS(*sample*)   **N**   *Statistic.* The uncorrected sum of squares.

VAR

VAR(*sample*)   **N**   *Statistic.* The variance.

VERIFY

VERIFY(*string, chars*)   **N**   Returns the location of the first character in the string that is not one of the characters listed. Otherwise, it returns 0.

Example VERIFY('AAAAA', 'AB') is 0.

WAKEUP

WAKEUP(*SAS time or SAS datetime*)   **N**   Suspends execution and displays a dialog box until the SAS time or SAS datetime, unless the SAS datetime is already passed. Returns the number of seconds execution was suspended. **Operating system** OS/2

WEEKDAY

WEEKDAY(*SAS date*)   **N**   Returns the weekday number, with Sunday=1, Saturday=7.

YEAR

YEAR(*SAS date*)   **N**   Returns the year.

YYQ

YEAR(*year, quarter*)   **N**   Returns the SAS date.

ZIPFIPS

ZIPFIPS(*ZIP code*)   **N**   Returns the FIPS state number.

ZIPNAME

ZIPNAME(*ZIP code*)   **$** 200/varies   Returns the state name in uppercase letters.

ZIPNAMEL

ZIPNAMEL(*ZIP code*)   **$** 200/varies   Returns the state name.

Example ZIPNAMEL('33333') is 'Florida'.

ZIPSTATE

ZIPSTATE(*ZIP code*)   **$** 200/2   Returns the two-letter postal code for the state.

Example ZIPSTATE('90125') is 'CA'.

17
CALL routines

CALL routines are executed in a separate statement in the data step. Like functions, they use a list of arguments. However, the arguments for CALL routines are often variables that are given a value by the CALL routine.

EXECUTE

CALL EXECUTE(*text*);   Resolves the macro expression that is contained in the character argument. Resulting SAS statements or tokens are executed immediately after the data step. **Release** 6.07+

LABEL

CALL LABEL(*variable, character variable*);   Assigns the variable's label to the character variable.

RANBIN

CALL RANBIN(*seed variable, n, P, random number variable*);   Generates a random number from a binomial distribution.

RANCAU

CALL RANCAU(*seed variable, random number variable*);   Generates a random number from a Cauchy distribution with $\alpha = 1$ and $\beta = 1$.

RANEXP

CALL RANEXP(*seed variable, random number variable*);   Generates a random number from an exponential distribution with $\lambda = 1$.

RANGAM

CALL RANGAM(*seed variable, a, random number variable*);   Generates a random number from a gamma distribution with $b = 1$. **Release** 6.06+

RANNOR

CALL RANNOR(*seed variable, random number variable*);   Generates a random number from a normal distribution with $\mu = 0$ and $\sigma = 1$.

RANPOI

CALL RANPOI(*seed variable, λ, random number variable*);   Generates a random number from a Poisson distribution.

RANTBL

CALL RANTBL(*seed variable, f(1), f(2), . . . , random number variable*);
Generates a random counting number from the indicated distribution.

RANTRI

CALL RANTRI(*seed variable, hypotenuse, random number variable*);
Generates a random number from a triangular distribution on the interval
[0, 1].

RANUNI

CALL RANUNI(*seed variable, random number variable*);   Generates a
random number from the uniform distribution on the interval [0, 1].

SOUND

CALL SOUND(*hertz, duration in 80ths of a second*);   Beeps.

SYMPUT

CALL SYMPUT(*macrovariable name, character value*);   Assigns the value
to the macrovariable.

SYSTEM

CALL SYSTEM(*command*);   Executes the operating system command.
Release 6.06+ **Mode** Ignored in batch mode in some operating systems

TSO

CALL TSO(*command*);   Executes the TSO command.
Operating system MVS **Mode** Foreground

VNAME

CALL VNAME(*variable name, character variable*);   Assigns the variable's
name to the character variable.

18

Base SAS procs

A proc is run by a proc step, which is a separate step in a SAS program. This chapter describes the syntax for base SAS procs. Procs also use the proc step statements described in chapter 6.

Most procs read input data from a SAS dataset that is identified by the DATA= term in the PROC statement. The default is DATA=_LAST_, the most recently created SAS dataset. Most procs can use the BY statement to divide the input SAS dataset into groups, and statements such as FORMAT and LABEL to modify attributes of variables.

A few procs always create an output SAS dataset, which is usually identified by the OUT= option on the PROC statement. For these procs, the default is OUT=_DATA_.

In a proc step, the RUN statement causes the preceding statements to be executed. This is usually the end of the step, but run-group procs, marked **RUN** in the entries, can have several RUN statements dividing the step into run groups.

APPEND

PROC APPEND DATA=*SAS dataset* OUT=*SAS dataset option*;

Copies a SAS dataset or appends the observations of one SAS dataset to another.

If the output SAS dataset does not already exist, the proc copies the input SAS dataset to the output SAS dataset. If the output SAS dataset exists and the input SAS dataset matches it closely enough, the proc copies the observations of the input SAS dataset to the end of the output SAS dataset.

Terms/Options

DATA= NEW= The input SAS dataset.

OUT= BASE= The output SAS dataset, to which observations are appended.

FORCE Drops or truncates input variables, if necessary.

CALENDAR

PROC CALENDAR DATA=*SAS dataset options*;
START *variable*;
optional statements

Prints a SAS dataset in the form of a monthly calendar.

Terms/Options

CALEDATA=*SAS dataset* Input calendar dataset that contains work schedules.

DATETIME Uses SAS datetime values instead of SAS date variables.

DAYLENGTH=*hours:minutes* For a schedule calendar, the length of the standard work day.

FILL Prints months with no input observations.

FORMCHAR='*characters*' FORMCHAR(*index ...*)='*characters*' Overrides all or selected characters of the FORMCHAR= system option.

HOLIDATA=*SAS dataset* Input SAS dataset defining holidays.

HEADER=SMALL *or* MEDIUM *or* LARGE 1-, 4-, or 7-line header.

INTERVAL=DAY *or* WORKDAY How durations are measured.

LEGEND Prints a box identifying variables that are printed.

MEANTYPE=NOBS *or* NDAYS Weight for calculating means.

MISSING Prints missing values, instead of ignoring them.

WEEKDAYS Does not print Saturdays and Sundays.

WORKDATA=*SAS dataset* An input workdays dataset that defines standard shifts.

Statements

START *variable*; The variable that contains the starting date of the activity. **Alias** STA, DATE, ID

DUR *variable*; The variable that contains the duration of the activity. **Alias** DURATION FIN *variable*; The variable that contains the concluding date of the activity. **Alias** FINISH

VAR *variables*; Variables to be displayed in the calendar. **Alias** VARIABLE

HOLISTART *variable*; The variable in the holiday dataset that contains the starting date of the holiday. **Alias** HOLISTA, HOLIDAY

HOLIDUR *variable*; The variable in the holiday dataset that contains the duration of the holiday. **Alias** HOLIDURATION

HOLIFIN *variable*; The variable in the holiday dataset that contains the concluding date of the holiday. **Alias** HOLIFINISH

HOLIVAR *variable*; The variable in the holiday dataset that contains the name of the holiday. **Alias** HOLIVARIABLE, HOLINAME

OUTSTART *day of week*; The starting day of the week. **Alias** OUTSTA

OUTDUR *n*; $1 \leq n \leq 7$ The number of days that are displayed in the week. **Alias** OUTDURATION OUTFIN *day of week*; The last day displayed in the week. **Alias** OUTFINISH

CALID *variable / option*; A group variable that identifies multiple output calendars. **Option** OUTPUT=SEPARATE *or* COMBINED *or* MIX **Default** CALID _CAL_ / OUTPUT=COMBINED;

MEAN *variables / optional* F *or* FORMAT=*format specification*; Displays means of these variables for each month.

SUM *variables / optional* F *or* FORMAT=*format specification*; Displays sums of these variables for each month.

CATALOG

PROC CATALOG CATALOG=*catalog* options;
  optional statements

Allows actions on entries in a catalog.   **RUN**

Terms/Options

CATALOG *or* CAT *or* C=*catalog* Identifies the catalog.

ENTRYTYPE *or* ET=*entry type* Restricts the additional statements in the
proc to one entry type.

KILL Deletes all entries in the catalog.

Statements

CHANGE *entry=new name . . . / option*; Changes the names of entries.
Option ET=*entry type*

CONTENTS *option*; Lists the catalog's entries. **Options** FILE=*fileref*
OUT=*SAS dataset*

COPY OUT=*catalog copy options entry option*; SELECT *or* EXCLUDE *entries /
entry option*;. Copies some or all entries. **Copy options** IN=*catalog*
MOVE Deletes after copying. NOEDIT Locks copies of some entry types.
NOSOURCE NOSRC Omits the program of a PROGRAM entry.
Entry option ET=*entry type*

DELETE *entry list / option*; *or* SAVE *entry list / option*; Deletes entries.
Option ET=*entry type*

EXCHANGE *entry=entry . . . / option*; Swaps the names of a pair of entries.
Option ET=*entry type*

MODIFY *entry* (DESCRIPTION='*label* '); Changes the description of an
entry. **Release** 6.07+

Examples

This step changes the name of WORK.MEDICAL.CLINIC.SCREEN to
WORK.MEDICAL.HOSPITAL.SCREEN and changes its description:

```
PROC CATALOG CATALOG=WORK.MEDICAL;
  CHANGE CLINIC.SCREEN=HOSPITAL.SCREEN;
  MODIFY HOSPITAL.SCREEN
    (DESCRIPTION='Clinical Data Entry Form');
QUIT;
```

This step copies only the PROGRAM and KEYS entries from the catalog
WORK.NHTRUST to the catalog DEV.NHTRUST:

```
PROC CATALOG CATALOG=WORK.NHTRUST;
  COPY OUT=DEV.NHTRUST ET=PROGRAM;
  COPY OUT=DEV.NHTRUST ET=KEYS;
```

CHART

PROC CHART DATA=*SAS dataset* options;
  optional statements

Produces charts using text characters.

Options

FORMCHAR(*index . . .*) = '*characters*' Overrides selected characters of the FORMCHAR= system option.

LPI=*ratio* Determines proportions. Use a value that is 10 times the ratio of character width to line height in your printer's output. The default is 6.0.

Statements

BLOCK *variables / chart options group options block chart options*; Creates a block chart.

HBAR *variables / chart options group options statistic options bar chart options*; Creates a horizontal bar chart.

PIE *variables / chart options*; Creates a pie chart.

STAR *variables / chart options*; Creates a star chart.

VBAR *variables / chart options group options bar chart options*; Creates a vertical bar chart.

Chart options

AXIS=*min max* AXIS=*max* AXIS=*list* Defines the axis range.

FREQ=*variable* Identifies the frequency variable.

LEVELS=*n* Number of midpoints for continuous variables.

MIDPOINTS=*list* Values of midpoints.

MISSING Includes missing values.

NOHEADER NOHEADING Suppresses header line (except in bar charts).

SYMBOL='*character(s)*' Symbols that are used to form bars and blocks (if subgroups are not used).

SUMVAR=*variable* Identifies variable to be analyzed.

TYPE= Identifies type of data to be charted. CFREQ Cumulative frequency. CPERCENT CPCT Cumulative percent. FREQ Frequency. MEAN Mean. PERCENT PCT Percent. SUM Sum.

Group options

DISCRETE Indicates the discrete chart variable.

GROUP=*variable* Produces side-by-side charts that are grouped by this variable.

G100 Each group is 100%.

NOSYMBOL NOLEGEND Suppresses the subgroup symbol table.

SUBGROUP=*variable* Subdivides bars to show groups defined by this variable.

Statistic options

CFREQ Prints the cumulative frequency.

CPERCENT Prints the cumulative percent.

FREQ Prints the frequency.

NOSTATS NOSTAT Suppresses statistics.

PERCENT Prints the percent.

SUM Prints total frequency.

Bar chart options

DESCENDING   Prints bars in descending order of size.

GSPACE=*n*   The space between groups. **Release** 6.07+

NOSPACE   Allows vertical bars with no space between them.

NOZEROS   Suppresses bars with zero frequencies.

REF=*number*   Draws a reference line.

REF=*number* . . .   Draws reference lines. **Release** 6.07+

SPACE=*n*   The space between bars. **Release** 6.07+

WIDTH=*n*   The width of bars. **Release** 6.07+

CIMPORT

PROC CIMPORT INFILE=*file   type=output file   options*;
Converts a transport file to a SAS file.

Terms/Options

INFILE=*file*   Identifies the input transport file.

LIBRARY *or* LIB=*libref*   CATALOG *or* CAT *or* C=*catalog*   DS *or* DATA= *SAS dataset*   Identifies the output library or SAS file.

ET=(*entry types*)   Imports selected entry types.
EET=(*entry types*)   Excludes selected entry types. **Release** 6.07+

NEDIT   Locks imported PROGRAM entries. NSRC   Omits source code from imported PROGRAM entries. **Release** 6.07+

NOCOMPRESS   Does not compress SAS data files and catalogs.

For SAS version 5 PROGRAM entries: OPT   Optimizes. NOOPT   Translates without optimizing. MODEV5   Does not translate.

SELECT *or* EXCLUDE=(*entries*)   When importing a catalog, it copies only some entries.

TAPE   Use for a sequential input file.

COMPARE

PROC COMPARE DATA=*SAS dataset options*;
   optional statements
Compares two SAS datasets or compares variables.

Options

DATA *or* BASE=*SAS dataset*   The SAS dataset to be compared to.

COMPARE *or* COMP *or* C=*SAS dataset*   The SAS dataset to be compared, if it is different from the DATA= SAS dataset.

OUT=*SAS dataset*   The output SAS dataset.

METHOD=ABSOLUTE *or* EXACT *or* RELATIVE *or* RELATIVE(*number*)   The comparison method.

ALLOBS ALLSTATS ALLVARS BRIEF CRITERION=*number* FUZZ=*number* LISTALL *or* LIST LISTBASE LISTBASEOBS LISTBASEVAR LISTCOMP LISTCOMPOBS LISTCOMPVAR LISTEQUALVAR LISTOBS LISTVAR MAXPRINT=*n or* (*n, n*) NODATE NOMISSBASE NOMISCOMP NOMISSING *or* NOMISS NOPRINT NOSUMMARY NOTE NOVALUES OUTALL OUTBASE OUTCOMP OUTDIF OUTNOEQUAL OUTPERCENT OUTSTATS=*SAS dataset* PRINTALL STATS TRANSPOSE WARNING *or* ERROR

Statements
ID *optional* DESCENDING *variable ... optional* NOTSORTED;   Variables that are used to match observations.

VAR *variables*;   Variables in the base dataset to be compared to.

WITH *variables*;   Variables in the comparison dataset to be compared, if they have different names.

Example
The step below compares the values of the variables TIME and ACCUR in the SAS dataset AFTER with the same variables in the SAS dataset BEFORE. Both SAS datasets are in sorted order by the variables DATE and NAME.

```
PROC COMPARE DATA=BEFORE COMPARE=AFTER METHOD=EXACT;
  ID DATE NAME;
  VAR TIME ACCUR;
RUN;
```

CONTENTS
PROC CONTENTS DATA=*SAS dataset or libref.*_ALL_ *options*;

Describes the contents of a SAS dataset.

Options
DIRECTORY Lists the members of the library that contains the SAS dataset.

DETAILS Also includes observation count, entry count, index, and label columns in the directory listing. NODETAILS Omits those columns.
Release 6.07+

MEMTYPE *or* MTYPE *or* MT=*member type or* (*member type, ...*) *or* ALL Selects one or more member types.

NODS Suppresses print output except for the directory page. NOPRINT Suppresses all print output.

OUT=*SAS dataset* Output SAS dataset, with one observation for each variable.

POSITION Also lists variables in order of position.

SHORT Lists variable names only.

CONVERT
PROC CONVERT BMDP=*fileref or* OSIRIS=*fileref* DICT=*fileref or*
  SPSS=*fileref options*;

Imports BMDP, OSIRIS, and SPSS files. **Operating system** Multiuser

Options FIRSTOBS=*n* OBS=*n* OUT=*SAS dataset*

COPY
PROC COPY IN=*libref* OUT=*libref options*;
  optional statement

Copies SAS files.

Terms/Options
INDEX=YES Copies indexes with SAS data files. INDEX=NO Does not copy indexes. **Release** 6.07+

MEMTYPE *or* MTYPE *or* MT=(*member types*)   Copies selected member types.

MOVE   Deletes after copying.

ALTER=*password*   The alter password if you use the MOVE option for alter-protected members.   **Release** 6.07+

Statements

SELECT *or* EXCLUDE *members / option*;   Copies selected members.
Options MEMTYPE *or* MTYPE *or* MT=(*member types*)

Example

This step copies all members of the SAS data library HERE to the SAS data library THERE:

```
 PROC COPY IN=HERE OUT=THERE INDEX=YES;
RUN;
```

CORR

```
 PROC CORR DATA=SAS dataset options;
  optional statements
```
Measures correlations.

Options ALPHA BEST=*n* COV CSSCP HOEFFDING OUTH=*SAS dataset*
KENDALL OUTK=*SAS dataset* NOCORR NOMISS NOPRINT NOPROB
NOSIMPLE PEARSON OUTP=*SAS dataset* RANK SINGULAR=*number*
SPEARMAN OUTS=*SAS dataset* SSCP
VARDEF=N *or* DF *or* WEIGHT *or* WGT *or* WDF

Statements

VAR *variables*;   Measures correlations of these variables.

WITH *variables*;   Measures correlations between these variables and the VAR variables.

PARTIAL *variables*;   Variables for partial correlation.

FREQ *variable*;   The frequency variable.

WEIGHT *variable*;   The weight variable.

CPORT

```
 PROC CPORT type=input file FILE=file options;
  optional statements
```
Creates a transport file.

Terms/Options

LIBRARY *or* LIB=*libref* CATALOG *or* CAT *or* C=*catalog* DATA *or* DS =*SAS dataset*   Identifies the input library or SAS file.

FILE=*file*   Identifies the output transport file.

AFTER=*SAS date*   Omits catalog entries that are not modified after this date.

ET=(*entry types*)   Imports selected entry types.
EET=(*entry types*)   Excludes selected entry types.   **Release** 6.07+

INDEX=YES   Copies indexes with SAS data files.   INDEX=NO   Does not copy indexes.   **Release** 6.07+

INTYPE=*DBCS type* or OUTTYPE=*DBCS type* or UPCASE

MEMTYPE or MTYPE or MT=*member type* or (*member type member type
...*) Copies selected member types.

NEDIT Locks exported PROGRAM entries. NSRC Omits source code
from exported PROGRAM entries. **Release** 6.07+

NOCOMPRESS Does not compress the transport file.

OUT=*libref* Also copies to this SAS data library.

SELECT or EXCLUDE=(*entries*) When exporting a catalog, it copies only
some entries.

TAPE Use for a sequential output transport file.

TRANSLATE=(*n* TO *n* ...) Translates characters.

Statement

TRANTAB NAME=*translation table options*; Uses the translation table to
translate characters in exported entries. **Options** Applies the translation
table to selected entry types: TYPE=(*entry types*) The listed entry types.
OPT=DISP Entries with windows.
OPT=SRC SOURCE entries OPT=(DISP SRC) Entries with windows and
SOURCE entries. **Release** 6.07+

DATASETS

PROC DATASETS *options member type option password options;
   optional statements*

Allows actions on members of a SAS data library. **RUN**

Options

LIBRARY=*libref* The SAS data library.

DETAILS Also includes observation count, entry count, index, and label
columns in the directory listing. NODETAILS Omits those columns.
Release 6.07+

FORCE Equivalent to the FORCE option in the APPEND statement.

KILL Deletes all members in the library.

NOLIST Does not write a list of members in the log.

NOWARN Continues executing even if a member that is named in a
statement is not found.

Member type option

MEMTYPE or MTYPE or MT=*member type* or (*member type,*...) or ALL
Selects member types to to be processed.

Statements

AGE *member member* ... / *member type option password option*;
Renames each member listed with the next name on the list and deletes
the last member in the list. The first member in the list should already
exist.

CHANGE *member=name* ... / *member type option password option*;
Renames the member.

EXCHANGE *member=member* ... / *member type option password option*;
Swaps the names of a pair of members.

APPEND DATA=*SAS dataset* OUT=*SAS dataset option*;   Equivalent to the APPEND proc.

CONTENTS DATA=*SAS dataset or libref._ALL_ options*;   Equivalent to the CONTENTS proc.

COPY OUT=*libref options; optional secondary statement*   Equivalent to the COPY proc.

DELETE *member list / member type option password option*; or SAVE *member list / member type option*;   Deletes members.

REPAIR *member password option*;   Attempts to repair a SAS data file or catalog.

MODIFY *member (dataset options); optional secondary statements*
Modifies a SAS data file. **Dataset options** LABEL= TYPE= *password option* SORTEDBY=*sort clause*

Secondary statements for MODIFY

RENAME *variable=name* ...;   Changes the name of a variable.

INFORMAT *variables informat specification* ...;   Changes the informat attribute of variables.

FORMAT *variables informat specification* ...;   Changes the format attribute of variables.

LABEL *variable='label'* ...;   Changes the label attribute of a variable.

INDEX CREATE *index or index=(variable variable...) ... / index options*;
Creates an index. **Index options** NOMISS   Omits observations with missing values for the key variables from the index. This kind of index is not used by the BY statement. UNIQUE   Prevents observations from being added that duplicate existing key values.

INDEX DELETE *index*...;   Deletes an index.

Examples

This step deletes all members of the WORK library:

```
 PROC DATASETS LIBRARY=WORK NOLIST KILL;
QUIT;
```

This step deletes LIVE.PRIOR, renames LIVE.CURRENT as LIVE.PRIOR, and renames LIVE.NEXT as LIVE.CURRENT:

```
 PROC DATASETS LIBRARY=LIVE;
  AGE NEXT CURRENT PRIOR / MT=DATA;
QUIT;
```

This step creates a simple index on the variable KEY in the SAS dataset BIG.BIGFILE and deletes the index on the variable OLDKEY:

```
 PROC DATASETS LIBRARY=BIG;
  MODIFY BIGFILE;
   INDEX CREATE KEY;
   INDEX DELETE OLDKEY;
QUIT;
```

This step changes the names of the variables STATE and L_NAME to TERR and LASTNAME in the SAS dataset PEOPLE.WEST:

```
PROC DATASETS LIBRARY=PEOPLE;
  MODIFY WEST;
    RENAME STATE=TERR L_NAME=LASTNAME;
QUIT;
```

DISPLAY

```
PROC DISPLAY CATALOG=entry;
```
Executes an AF entry. **Release** 6.07+

EXPLODE

```
PROC EXPLODE;
PARMCARDS or PARMCARDS4;
parameter lines
; or ;;;;
```
Prints oversized text using regular text characters. **Release** 6.07+

Parameter lines

L
Forms characters out of asterisks. This is the default.

D
Forms darker characters by overprinting H, Q, and T.

Sn
Skips *n* lines.

P
Starts a new page.

n message
Skips *n* lines and prints the message. The message can contain capital letters and commonly used symbols. Use the PARMCARDS4 statement if the message contains a semicolon.

U *characters*
Forms an underline out of asterisks. Any nonblank character prints as an underline.

Example

```
PROC EXPLODE;
PARMCARDS;
D
5ROCK & ROLL
5  4 EVER
U  4 EVER
;
```

FORMAT

```
PROC FORMAT options;
  optional statements
```
Defines and prints formats and informats. **RUN**

Options

LIBRARY=*libref* The library in which the formats and informats are stored in a catalog called FORMATS.

LIBRARY=*catalog* A catalog in which the formats and informats are stored. **Release** 6.07+

FMTLIB Prints the contents of the FORMATS catalog.
PAGE Prints each entry on a separate page.

CNTLIN=*SAS dataset* The input control dataset. Informats and formats that are defined by the dataset are added to the FORMATS catalog.

CNTLOUT=*SAS dataset* The output control dataset. Entries in the FORMATS catalog are converted to a SAS dataset format.

MAXLABELEN=*n* The maximum label length that is printed or written to a SAS dataset. **Release** 6.07+

MAXSELEN=*n* The maximum range value length that is printed or written to a SAS dataset. **Release** 6.07+

NOTSORTED Stores ranges in the order you specify, rather than in sorted order. **Release** 6.07+

NOREPLACE Does not replace existing catalog entries. **Release** 6.07+

Statements

SELECT *entries*; or EXCLUDE *entries*; Reads selected entries from the FORMATS catalog.

INVALUE *informat* (*informat options*) *range* = *value* ...; Defines a value informat.

VALUE *format* (*format options*) *range* = *value* ...; Defines an value format.

PICTURE *format* (*format options*) *range* = *picture* (*picture options*) ...; Defines an picture format.

Ranges

For character formats, character informats, and numeric informats through release 6.06, ranges consist of character values. For numeric formats, ranges consist of numeric values. For numeric informats beginning in release 6.07, ranges can include numeric and character values.

value
value - *value*
value or LOW   - *or* -< *or* <- *or* <-<   *value or* HIGH
OTHER
range, range, . . .

Format options

DEFAULT=*n* Default width of the format.

MAX=*n* Maximum width of the format.

MIN=*n* Minimum width of the format.

FUZZ=*number* Extends ranges by the amount specified. **Default** 1E-12

ROUND For picture formats only, it rounds the numeral instead of truncating it. **Release** 6.07+

Informat options

DEFAULT=*n* The default width of the informat.

MAX=*n* The maximum width of the informat.

MIN=*n* The minimum width of the informat.

UPCASE Converts the input value to uppercase before comparing it to the ranges. **Release** 6.06+

JUST Removes leading blanks from the input value before comparing it to the ranges. **Release** 6.06+

Special informat values

SAME Unchanged or treated as ordinary numeric data.

ERROR Treated as invalid data.

Pictures

A *picture* is a character constant that contains digits and other characters. The first character is the picture is a digit. Digits in the picture are *digit selectors*, which represent a position for a digit or fill character in the formatted value. *Fill characters* are used only for zero digit selectors at the beginning of the picture. Any other characters in the picture are literal characters that appear in the formatted value. A picture is simply a literal value if it does not contain any digits or if the NOEDIT option is used.

Picture options

FILL='*character*' The fill character: replaces digit selector zeroes at the beginning of the picture if the numeral has fewer digits than the number of digit selectors. **Default** FILL=' '

MULTIPLIER *or* MULT=*factor* The value is multiplied by this factor before being converted to a numeral.

NOEDIT The picture is treated as a literal value.

Example
```
PROC FORMAT;
  INFORMAT TIX
    0-5=0
    6-17, 60-HIGH=2.00
    OTHER=4.00;
  FORMAT SIGN (MIN=1)
    LOW-<0 = 'NEGATIVE'
    0 = 'ZERO'
    0<-HIGH = 'POSITIVE'
    ._-.Z = 'UNKNOWN';
RUN;
```

FORMS
```
PROC FORMS DATA=SAS dataset options;
  optional statement
  LINE n variables / options; ...
```
Prints data in rectangular blocks. Each observation from the input SAS dataset is printed in the same rectangular form.

Options

ACROSS *or* A=*n* The number of form units across the page.

ALIGN=*n* Prints a number of form units that are filled with Xs.

BETWEEN *or* B=*n* The horizontal space between form units.

COPIES *or* C=*n* Prints each observation n times.

DOWN *or* D=*n* Skips *n* lines at the top of the page.

FILE *or* DDNAME *or* DD=*fileref* Prints to the specified file.

CC Uses carriage-control characters.

INDENT *or* I=*n* The left margin.

LINES *or* L=*n* The number of lines in a form unit.

NDOWN *or* ND=*n* The number of form units that are printed down the page.

PAGESIZE *or* P=*n* The number of lines on the page.

SETS=*n* Prints the entire output *n* times.

SKIP *or* S=*n* The vertical spacing between form units.

WIDTH *or* W=*n* The width of a form unit.

Statements

FREQ *variable*; Identifies a frequency variable, which indicates the number of times to print each observation.

LINE *n variables / options*; Prints the variables on the indicated line of the form unit. **Options** INDENT *or* I=n Indents the line. LASTNAME *or* L Puts the words after the comma at the beginning. PACK *or* P Removes trailing blanks from variable values. REMOVE *or* R Omits the line if the variables are missing or blank.

Example

This step could be used to print addresses on mailing labels:

```
 PROC FORMS DATA=MAILING.LIST
   ACROSS=3 LINES=6 DOWN=3;
   LINE 1 FIRSNAME LASTNAME / PACK;
   LINE 2 ADDRESS;
   LINE 3 CITY ST ZIP;
RUN;
```

FREQ

```
 PROC FREQ DATA=SAS dataset options;
   optional statements
```

Prints tables of frequencies. The tables show the number of observations in the input SAS dataset that have each value of a variable or combination of variables.

Options

FORMCHAR(1, 2, 7)='*chars*' Overrides characters of the FORMCHAR= system option.

ORDER=DATA Prints output values in their order of appearance in the input data. ORDER=INTERNAL Prints values in sorted order.
ORDER=EXTERNAL Prints in sorted order of the formatted values.
ORDER=FREQ Prints in descending order of frequency.

PAGE Prints only one table on a page.

NOPRINT Suppresses print output. **Release** 6.07+

Statements

FREQ *variable*; Identifies a frequency variable.

TABLES *requests / options*; Prints tables.

OUTPUT OUT=*SAS dataset statistics*;   Creates an output SAS dataset from the last table request. **Statistics** AJCHI BDCHI CMHCOR CMHGA CMHRMS CONTGY CRAMV EXACT GAMMA KENTB LAMCR LAMDAS LAMRC LGOR LGRRC1 LGRRC2 LRCHI MHCHI MHOR MHRRC1 MHRRC2 N NMISS PCHI PCORR PHI PLCORR RRC1 RRC2 RROR SCORR SMDCR SMDRC STUTC U UCR URC   **Statistic groups** ALL CHISQ CMH CMH1 CMH2 MEASURES **Release** 6.07+

Requests

A *table request* consists of one variable or a combination of variables that are separated by asterisks. For a two-way table, the first variable forms rows. The last variable forms columns. You can also use variable lists in parentheses to define multiple tables.

TABLES statement options

LIST   Prints in list format.

MISSING   Uses missing values.

MISSPRINT   Prints missing value frequencies in tables.

OUT=*SAS dataset*   Creates a SAS dataset from the last table that is requested.

NOPRINT   Does not print tables.

OUTPCT   Includes percent variables in the output SAS dataset. **Release** 6.07+

SPARSE   Uses all possible combinations, even those that do not appear in the data.

TOTPCT   Prints percent of total in tables with more than two dimensions. **Release** 6.07+

Statistics: ALL ALPHA=*number* CELLCHI2 CHISQ CMH CMH1 CMH2 CUMCOL DEVIATION EXACT EXPECTED MEASURES NOCOL NOCUM NOFREQ NOPERCENT PLCORR SCORES=MODRIDIT *or* RANK *or* RIDIT *or* TABLE

Examples

This step prints a separate frequency table for each variable in the SAS dataset SUBJECTS:

```
 PROC FREQ DATA=SUBJECTS;
RUN;
```

The step below prints three two-way frequency tables, which combine the variable CLASS (which forms rows) with each of the variables SCORE1, SCORE2, and SCORE3 (which form columns).

```
 PROC FREQ DATA=SUBJECTS;
   TABLES CLASS*(SCORE1-SCORE3);
RUN;
```

MEANS

Equivalent to the SUMMARY proc with the PRINT option as the default, with this exception: if you omit the VAR statement, all numeric variables are used.

Example

This step prints several descriptive statistics for all numeric variables in the SAS dataset SUBJECTS:

```
PROC MEANS DATA=SUBJECTS;
RUN;
```

OPTIONS

```
PROC OPTIONS options;
```

Lists values of system options.

Options

SHORT LONG

HOST PORTABLE *or* NOHOST OPTION=*option name* **Release** 6.07+

PDS

```
PROC PDS DDNAME=file  options;
  optional statements
```

Allows actions on members of a PDS. **Operating system** MVS

Options

NOLIST Suppresses the list of PDS members.

KILL Deletes all members of the PDS.

Statements

DELETE *member*...; Deletes PDS members.

CHANGE *member=name* ...; Changes the names of PDS members.

EXCHANGE *member=member* ...; Swaps names of pairs of PDS members.

PDSCOPY

```
PROC PDSCOPY INDD=file  OUTDD=file  options;
  optional statement
```

Copies a PDS. **Operating system** MVS

Options ALIASMATCH=BOTH *or* EITHER *or* NAME *or* TTR BLKSIZE=*n* DC
DCBS *or* NODCBS INTAPE MAXBLK=*n* NE NEWMOD NOALIAS *or* NOA
NOREPLACE *or* NOR NOTEST OUTTAPE SHAREINPUT *or* SHAREIN

Statements

SELECT *or* EXCLUDE *PDS members*; Copies selected PDS members.

PLOT

```
PROC PLOT DATA=SAS dataset  page options;
  PLOT request.../ plot options;
```

Produces scatter graphs using text characters. **RUN**

Page options

FORMCHAR(*index*...) Overrides one or more characters of the FORMCHAR= system option.

HPERCENT=*percent* VPERCENT=*percent* The width and height of each plot as a percent of the page width and height. Allows more than one plot per page.

MISSING Uses blank values in determining axes. **Release** 6.07+

NOLEGEND Suppresses the legend.

NOMISS Ignores missing values in determining axes.

UNIFORM Scales axes the same way for all BY groups.

VTOH=*ratio* The aspect ratio. Use the ratio of the line height to the width of a character that is printed by your printer.

Requests

vertical variable ⋆horizontal variable

vertical variable or (*variables*)
    optional : *or* ⋆ *horizontal variable or* (*variables*)
    optional $ *label variable*   **Release** 6.07+
    optional ='*plot character*' *or plot variable*

List operators

(*list*) ⋆ (*list*) Creates all possible combinations of items in the lists.

(*list*) : (*list*) Combines items one by one. **Release** 6.07+

Plot options BOX CONTOUR CONTOUR=*n* HAXIS=*n* . . .
HAXIS=*start* TO *stop* BY *interval* HAXIS=BY *interval* HEXPAND HPOS=*n*
HREF=*n* . . . HREF=*start* TO *stop* BY *interval* HREFCHAR='*char*' HREVERSE
HSPACE=*n* HZERO LIST LIST=*penalty* OVERLAY
PENALTY(*index* . . .)=*penalty* . . . PLACEMENT *or* PLACE=(*label placement*)
S='*chars*' S*n*='*chars*' SLIST='*chars*' . . . SPLIT='*char*' STATES
VAXIS=*n* . . . VAXIS=*start* TO *stop* BY *interval* VAXIS=BY *interval*
VPOS=*n* VREF=*n* . . . VREF=*start* TO *stop* BY *interval* VREFCHAR='*char*'
VREVERSE VSPACE=*n* VZERO

Example

This step plots X against Y and X against Z on the same pair of axes:

```
PROC PLOT DATA=SPACE;
  PLOT Y⋆X='Y' Z⋆X='Z' / OVERLAY;
RUN;
```

PMENU

```
PROC PMENU options;
  MENU entry name;
  ITEM statements
  other statements
```

Defines a PMENU entry. **Release** 6.06+ **RUN**

Options

CATALOG=*catalog* The PMENU entry is stored in this catalog.

DESC '*description*' A description that is stored with the PMENU entry.

MENU statement

MENU *name*; Begins the definition of a menu. The first statement in a run group is a MENU statement that names the PMENU entry and defines a menu bar. Subsequent MENU statements define pull-down menus.

ITEM statement

Each MENU statement is immediately followed by ITEM statements, which define menu items. The order of the ITEM statements determines the order of menu items.

ITEM *'name'* or *name* *options*; Defines a menu item.

Options

SELECTION=*selection* MENU=*menu* DIALOG=*dialog box* Associates the menu item with a subsequent SELECTION, MENU, or DIALOG statement, which defines the action taken when the item is selected. GRAY Indicates that the menu item is inactive.

ACCELERATE='*char*' A character that can be typed in the menu to select the menu item.

MNEMONIC='*char*' A character that can be typed as the equivalent of selecting the menu item.

SEPARATOR statement

The SEPARATOR statement can be used between any two ITEM statements to define a separator line.

SEPARATOR; Defines a separator line.

SELECTION statement

SELECTION *selection* '*string*' or *command*; Defines a command string that results from selecting a menu item.

DIALOG statement

The DIALOG statement and subsequent TEXT, CHECKBOX, RADIOBOX, and RBUTTON statements define a dialog box.

DIALOG *dialog box* '*command string*' *optional* HELP='*entry*'; Defines a dialog box. The command string results when the user presses the OK button in the dialog box; no action results when the user presses the Cancel button. The command string can contain symbols that represent values from text boxes, check boxes, and radio boxes in the dialog box:

@*n* The value from text box *n*.

%*n* The value from radio box *n*.

&*n* The value from check box *n*.

TEXT statement

TEXT #*line* @*column* '*text*' *options*; Displays a message in the dialog box.

TEXT #*line* @*column* LEN=*length* *options*; Defines a text box, where the user can enter a text value.

Options

COLOR=*color* The color of the text.

ATTR=HIGHLIGH or BLINK or REV_VIDE or UNDERLIN The video attribute of the text.

CHECKBOX statement

A check box represents an on/off choice.

CHECKBOX *optional* ON #*line* @*column* '*text*' *options*; Defines a check box. The text is displayed next to the check box. If the check box is checked, the text is substituted in the dialog box's command string.

Options

ON The check box is checked by default.

COLOR=*color* The color of the text.

SUBSTITUTE='*text*' This text is substituted in the dialog box command string, in place of the displayed text, if the check box is checked. **Release** 6.07+

RADIOBOX and RBUTTON statements

A radio box consists of radio buttons. The user selects one radio button in the radio box.

RADIOBOX DEFAULT=*n*;
RBUTTON *optional* NONE *#line* @*column* '*text*' *options*; ...

Defines a radio box. The radio button that is defined by the indicated RBUTTON statement is selected by default.

Options

NONE The radio button indicates no selection from the radio box.

COLOR=*color* Color.

SUBSTITUTE='*text*' This text is substituted in the dialog box command string, in place of the displayed text, if the radio button is selected. **Release** 6.07+

Example

This step defines a menu bar with the items Large, Small, and End — each associated with a display manager command:

```
PROC PMENU CATALOG=WORK.DEV DESC 'Alice in Wonderland';
  MENU RESIZE;
  ITEM 'Large' SELECTION=LARGE;
  ITEM 'Small' SELECTION=SMALL;
  ITEM 'End';
  SELECTION LARGE  'WDEF 2 2 20 78';
  SELECTION SMALL  'WDEF 8 20 9 40';
QUIT;
```

PRINT

PROC PRINT DATA=*SAS dataset options*;
optional statements

Prints a SAS dataset in table form, with observations as rows and variables as columns.

Options

DOUBLE D Double-spaces.

LABEL L Uses variable labels. SPLIT='*char*' Uses labels and splits them wherever this character appears in the label.

N Prints the number of observations.

NOOBS Suppresses the observation number column.

ROUND Rounds numbers to two decimal places or to the number of decimal places in the variable's format attribute.

UNIFORM U Uses the same spacing on all pages.

HEADING=*direction*   *direction*: HORIZONTAL H VERTICAL V The orientation of column headings. **Release** 6.07+

ROWS=PAGE Prints only one row of variables per page, even if more than one row is required. **Release** 6.07+

Column width: WIDTH=FULL The variable's formatted width.
WIDTH=UNIFORM *or* U The formatted width if the variable has a format with an explicit width; otherwise, the longest formatted value.
WIDTH=UNIFORMBY *or* UBY The formatted width if the variable has a format with an explicit width; otherwise, the longest formatted value in the BY group. WIDTH=MINIMUM *or* MIN The longest formatted value on the page. **Release** 6.07+

Statements

ID *variables*; Prints these variables at the left side of the line.

VAR *variables*; Prints these variables. If there is no VAR statement, all variables are printed.

SUM *variables*; Prints these variables and the totals for them.

SUMBY *variable*; Prints the subtotals at the end of a BY group for this BY variable and for any preceding BY variable.

PAGEBY *variable*; Starts a new page at the end of a BY group for this BY variable.

Examples

This step prints all the variables of the most recently created SAS dataset in the PRINT proc's default format, including a column of observation numbers at the left side:

```
 PROC PRINT;
RUN;
```

The step below prints selected variables, with MILE_OUT in the left column, formed into groups by the variables SIZE and CAR; each new value of SIZE starts on a separate page. It prints totals of the variables MILEAGE and PRICE for each value of CAR and SIZE, and for the SAS dataset as a whole. The report begins on page 1, with a title line at the top of each page.

```
OPTIONS PAGENO=1 NODATE CENTER;
TITLE1 'Autos 2 Go';
 PROC PRINT DATA=RENTAL LABEL;
   BY SIZE CAR;
   ID MILE_OUT;
   VAR MILEAGE  PRICE  DATE_OUT PT_OUT DATE_IN PT_IN;
   PAGEBY SIZE;
   SUM MILEAGE PRICE;
   SUMBY CAR;
   FORMAT MILE_OUT Z5. MILEAGE 6.2 PRICE DOLLAR7.2
     DATE_OUT DATE_IN MMDDYY8.;
   LABEL SIZE='Size Class' CAR='Car' MILE_OUT='Mileage At Pickup'
     MILEAGE='Distance' PRICE='Price'
     DATE_OUT='Pickup Date' DATE_IN='Dropoff Date'
     PT_OUT='Pickup Location' PT_IN='Dropoff Location';
RUN;
```

PRINTTO

```
 PROC PRINTTO options;
```
Redirects the log or standard print file. **Release** 6.06+

Options

LOG=*file* Redirects the log.

PRINT *or* FILE *or* NAME=*file* Redirects the standard print file.

UNIT=*nn* Redirects the standard print file to fileref FT*nn*F001.

NEW Replaces the contents of the file.

LOG=*entry* Redirects the log to a catalog entry of type LOG or OUTPUT. **Release** 6.07+

PRINT=*entry* Redirects the standard print file to a catalog entry of the type OUTPUT or LOG. **Release** 6.07+

LABEL='*label*' Provides a descriptive label for the catalog entry or entries. **Release** 6.07+

LOG=LOG PRINT=PRINT Restores the defaults.

Example

These statements identify a print file and redirect standard print output to it:

```
FILENAME LISTING2 'MEANS.LST';
 PROC PRINTTO PRINT=LISTING2;
RUN;
```

RANK

```
PROC RANK DATA=SAS dataset OUT=SAS dataset options;
 VAR variables;
 optional RANKS variables;
```

Ranks values of numeric variables.

Options

DESCENDING Ranks from largest to smallest. The default is from smallest to largest.

FRACTION F Fractional ranks, with 1 as the highest rank.
FN1 N1 NPLUS1 Fractional ranks, between 0 and 1.
PERCENT Fractional ranks times 100, with 100 as the highest rank.

GROUPS=*n* Divides values into *n* groups and assigns quantile ranks from 0 to $n - 1$.

TIES=HIGH *or* MEAN *or* LOW Decides ranks of tied values. The default is TIES=MEAN. For fractional ranks, the default is TIES=HIGH.

NORMAL=BLOM *or* TUKEY *or* WV Computes normal scores.
SAVAGE Computes Savage scores.

Statements

VAR *variables*; Ranks these variables.

RANKS *variables*; Keeps the VAR variables in the output SAS dataset and uses these new variable names for the rank variables.

Examples

This step ranks observations by increasing order of TIME to create the variable FINISH:

```
PROC RANK DATA=RACE.TIMES OUT=RACE.ORDER TIES=LOW;
```

```
    VAR TIME;
    RANKS FINISH;
RUN;
```

This step converts the variable APTITUDE to percentile ranks:

```
 PROC RANK DATA=SCORES OUT=PCTILE GROUPS=100;
   VAR APTITUDE;
RUN;
```

RELEASE
 PROC RELEASE DDNAME=*file* *options*;

Releases unused space at the end of a file. **Operating system** MVS

Options TOTAL=*n* TRACKS=*n* UNUSED=*n* RELEASE=*n* EXTENT BOUNDARY *or* TYPE=DSCB *or* CYL *or* TRK *or* ALLOC

REPORT
 PROC REPORT DATA=*SAS dataset options*;
   optional statements

Prints or summarizes a SAS dataset in table format. **Release** 6.07+

Options

CENTER Centers the report. NOCENTER Left-aligns the report.

COLWIDTH=*n* The default column width. The default is COLWIDTH=9.

HEADLINE Draws a horizontal line under the column headers.

HEADSKIP Leaves a blank line under the column headers.

LS=*n* The line size: the number of characters that are used on a line.

MISSING Treats missing values as valid values of CLASS variables.

NOHEADER Omits column headers. NAMED Omits column headers and writes the column name and an equals sign before each value in the report.

PANELS=*n* The page is divided horizontally into this many panels. The default is PANELS=1.

PS=*n* The page size: the number of lines used on a page.

PSPACE=*n* The horizontal spacing between panels. The default is PSPACE=4.

REPORT=*entry* A REPT entry that is used to format the report.

SHOWALL Displays all columns.

SPACING=*n* The horizontal spacing between columns.

SPLIT='*char*' Splits column headings wherever this character appears. The default is SPLIT='/'.

WRAP Wraps, if necessary, to display all columns together.

LIST Writes the report definition in the log.

OUTREPT=*entry* Stores the report definition in this REPT entry.

WINDOWS WD Opens the REPORT window for interactive report display or modification. PROMPT Opens the REPORT window and displays prompts. NOWINDOWS NOWD Does not open the REPORT window.

COMMAND   Displays command lines instead of action bars.

HELP=*catalog*   The catalog that contains help entries, which can be CBT and/or HELP entries, for the report.

NORKEYS   Closes the RKEYS window.

PROFILE=*catalog*   The catalog that contains the REPORT profile in the entry REPORT.PROFILE.   The default is PROFILE=SASUSER.PROFILE.

Statements

BY *variable*;   Produces a separate report for each BY group. You cannot use this statement with the REPORT window.

COLUMN *columns . . .*;   Defines the columns of the report.

BREAK BEFORE *or* AFTER *break variable / break options*;   Defines lines at the beginning or end of each group of observations that is defined by a value of the break variable. The break variable can be either a group variable or an order variable.

RBREAK BEFORE *or* AFTER / *break options*;   Defines lines at the beginning or end of the report.

DEFINE *item name / item options*;   Defines characteristics of an item in the report. The item can be a variable, statistic, or alias.

COMPUTE *computed variable / type option*; *code segment* ENDCOMP;   A COMPUTE block that is executed to assign values for a computed variable column. **Type option** LENGTH=*n* $1 \le n \le 200$ The computed variable is a character variable of length *n*. The default length is 8. CHARACTER CHAR The computed variable is a character variable. The default type is numeric.

COMPUTE BEFORE *or* AFTER *break variable code segment* ENDCOMP;   A COMPUTE block that is executed at the beginning of each group that is defined by the break variable. The break variable can be an order or group variable. The COMPUTE block can be used to write break lines.

COMPUTE BEFORE *or* AFTER *code segment* ENDCOMP;   A COMPUTE block that is executed at the beginning or end of the report.

FREQ *variable*;   The frequency variable.

WEIGHT *variable*;   The weight variable.

Column definitions

variable A column that displays a variable.

statistic A column that displays a statistic.

variable, statistic or statistic, variable   A column that displays a statistic computed for a variable.

column definition=alias Defines an alias for use in the DEFINE statement.

(*list*), (*list*) Multiple columns that combine every item in the first list with every item in the second list.

('*header*' . . . *column definitions*) A header that spans multiple columns.

Break options

COLOR=*color* The color of text in the break line.

OL Overline. DOL Double overline.

PAGE   Page break.

SKIP A blank line appears after the break lines.

SUMMARIZE A summary line that contains statistics and/or computed variables is written.

SUPPRESS The break variable is omitted from the break line.

UL Underline. **DUL** Double underline.

Item options

DISPLAY The variable is displayed as a column in the report. **ORDER** The variable determines the order of rows. **GROUP** The variable determines the order of rows and forms groups. The entire group is summarized and displayed as one row, if possible. **ACROSS** The variable forms groups. The entire group is summarized and displayed as a column. **ANALYSIS** Statistics are computed on the variable. **COMPUTED** A variable defined in a COMPUTE block.

statistic The statistic to be calculated for an analysis variable. The default statistic is SUM.

ORDER= How an order, group, or across variable is sorted: **DATA** In order of appearance in the input SAS dataset. **INTERNAL** In sorted order of values. **FORMATTED** In sorted order of formatted values. **FREQ** In descending order of frequency.

DESCENDING Reverses the sort order of an order, group, or across variable.

FLOW Word wraps when values are longer than the width of the column.

SPACING=*n* The horizontal spacing to the left of the column.

WIDTH=*n* The column width.

FORMAT=*format specification*

Alignment of the item and its heading: **LEFT** **CENTER** **RIGHT**

ITEMHELP=*entry name* The name of the CBT or HELP entry that is used as a help window for the item.

NOPRINT The column does not appear in the report. **NOZERO** The column appears only if it contains a nonzero, nonmissing value.

PAGE The column starts on a new page.

Code segments

A COMPUTE block begins with a COMPUTE statement and ends with an ENDCOMP statement. The statements in between are called a *code segment*.

A code segment can include any of these data step statements:

Assignment	LENGTH
CALL	LINK, RETURN
Comment	Null
DO, END	SELECT, WHEN, OTHERWISE, END
GOTO	Sum
IF . . . THEN, ELSE	

A code segment can also use LINE statements:

LINE *terms*; Writes a line in the report. **Terms** @*n* Moves the pointer to column *n*. **+***n* Advance the pointer by *n* columns. *variable format specification* Writes the variable. *'string'* Writes the string. *n*∗*'string'* Writes the string *n* times.

You can use these kinds of variable references in a code segment:

variable A group, order, display, or computed variable, or a variable that is created in a code segment.

variable.statistic An analysis variable.

_Cn_ The value in column *n*. Use this form for columns that are headed by across variables.

COL The column number of the computed variable.

A computed variable code segment can only use values that are associated with columns that appear to its left in the report and variables from previous code segments. You can compute code-segment variables in one or more code segments and then use them in a later code segment. The order of execution of the report and any code segments in it is from top to bottom and left to right.

An additional CALL routine can be used in code segments:

CALL DEFINE('*column*' or *column number*, '*attribute*', *value*); Sets the value of an attribute. The change applies only to the current row. Valid combinations of attribute and value arguments are:

> 'FORMAT', '*format specification*'
> 'COLOR', '*color*'
> 'HIGHLIGHT', 1 *or* 0
> 'BLINK', 1 *or* 0
> 'RVSVIDEO', 1 *or* 0
> 'COMMAND', '*command string*'

SORT
PROC SORT DATA=*SAS dataset options*;
  BY *optional* DESCENDING *variable*   ...;
Sorts the observations in a SAS dataset.

Options

OUT=*SAS dataset* The output SAS dataset. By default, the input SAS dataset is sorted in place.

FORCE Allows the use of options to delete variables and observations while sorting in place.

EQUALS Keeps observations with the same BY variable values in the same order. NOEQUALS Does not necessarily keep observations with the same BY variable values in the same order.

NODUPKEY Does not write multiple observations with the same BY variable values to the output SAS dataset.

NODUPLICATES NODUPREC NODUP Does not write consecutive identical observations to the output SAS dataset.

REVERSE Reverses the sort order of character variables.

Optional collating sequences: ASCII EBCDIC NORWEGIAN DANISH SWEDISH FINNISH NATIONAL

SORTSIZE=*n or nK or* MAX The amount of memory that is used for sorting.

TAGSORT Uses a tag sort algorithm: it sorts the BY variables first, then it sorts the rest of the variables. This is often more efficient.

Example

This step creates a sorted copy of the SAS dataset US, called USSORT:

```
 PROC SORT DATA=US OUT=USSORT;
  BY ASTRSIGN;
RUN;
```

SPELL

 PROC SPELL WORDLIST *or* IN=*text file or catalog or entry* *options*;
Checks spelling in a file that contains text. **Release** 6.06+

Terms/Options

VERIFY Checks spelling. This is the default. CREATE Creates a dictionary. UPDATE Adds words to a dictionary.

DICTIONARY=(*dictionary* ...) The dictionary that is being used.

NOMASTER Does not use the master dictionary.

SIZE=*n* The size in bytes of a dictionary that is being created.

SUGGEST Suggests alternatives for unrecognized words.

SQL

 PROC SQL *options*;
  SQL statements, RESET statements, and global statements
Executes SQL statements. **Release** 6.06+

Essential SQL terms

Table: SAS data file. Row: observation. Column: variable.

Options

After an SQL error: ERRORSTOP Stops executing SQL statements. NOERRORSTOP Continues execution with the next statement.

EXEC Executes SQL statements. NOEXEC Checks syntax only.

FEEDBACK Displays expanded statements. NOFEEDBACK Does not display expanded statements,

INOBS=*n* Limits the number of rows that are used from any one input source in a statement.

LOOPS=*n* Limits the repetitions of the innermost SQL loop.

OUTOBS=*n* Limits the number of output rows in any statement or expression.

PROMPT In an interactive session, it prompts the user when the INOBS=, OUTOBS=, or LOOPS= limit is reached.
NOPROMPT Stops executing when the limit is reached. This is the default.
Release 6.07+

NUMBER The SELECT statement generates a column ROW with row numbers. NONUMBER The SELECT statement does not use row numbers.

PRINT The results of the SELECT statement are printed. NOPRINT The results of the SELECT statement are not printed.

SORTSEQ=*collating sequence* The collating sequence that is used by an ORDER BY clause.

STIMER The proc times each SQL statement. NOSTIMER The proc times the step as a whole.

FLOW FLOW=*n* FLOW=*n n2* NOFLOW Controls text flow of character columns that are wider than *n*. **Release** 6.07+

DOUBLE Double-spaces print output. NODOUBLE Single-spaces. This is the default. **Release** 6.07+

UNDO_POLICY=NONE *or* OPTIONAL *or* REQUIRED The recovery strategy when errors occur in table updates. **Release** 6.07+

Statements

RESET *options*; Changes options.

ALTER TABLE *table* ADD *column definition, ...* *and/or* MODIFY *column definition, ...* *and/or* DROP *column, ...*; Adds columns, changes column attributes, or drops columns.

CREATE TABLE *table (column definition, ...)*; CREATE TABLE *table* LIKE *table*; Creates a new table with no rows.

CREATE TABLE *table* AS *query expression*; Creates a new table.

CREATE VIEW *view* AS *query expression*; Creates a new view.

CREATE VIEW *view* AS *query expression* ORDER BY *column, ...*; Creates a new sorted view.

CREATE *optional* UNIQUE INDEX *index* ON *table (column, ...)*; Creates an index.

DELETE FROM *table* WHERE *expression*; Conditionally deletes rows from a table.

DESCRIBE VIEW *view*; Describes an SQL view.

DESCRIBE TABLE *table*; Describes an SQL table. **Release** 6.07+

DROP TABLE *table, ...*; Deletes tables.

DROP VIEW *view, ...*; Deletes views.

DROP INDEX *index, ...* FROM *table*; Deletes indexes.

INSERT INTO *table or table(column, ...)* SET *column=expression, ...* *... or* VALUES (*value, ...*) *... or query expression*;. Adds rows to a table.

query expression optional ORDER BY *column, ...*; SELECT statement: prints the results of a query.

UPDATE *table* SET *column=expression, ... optional* WHERE *expression*; Changes the values in a table.

VALIDATE *query expression*; Checks the syntax of a query expression.

Essential SQL components (simplified)

column definition: name type optional (*width*) *optional attributes* *type*: NUMERIC, CHARACTER, etc.
attributes: INFORMAT= *...* , FORMAT= *...* , LABEL= *...*

query expression: SELECT *column(s), ...* FROM *table or view or equivalent expression optional* WHERE *expression*

Examples

These SQL statements create tables that contain data from the table ORIGINAL:

```
CREATE TABLE COPY AS SELECT * FROM ORIGINAL;
CREATE TABLE SUBSET AS
   SELECT * FROM ORIGINAL
   WHERE SELECT = 'Y';
```

This SQL statement creates a simple index on the variable NAME in the table PRODUCT.MASTER:

```
CREATE INDEX NAME ON PRODUCT.MASTER(NAME);
```

This SQL statement prints selected data from the table PRODUCT.MASTER:

```
SELECT NAME, LIST, ORIGINAL, SALE, CLERNC
   FROM PRODUCT.MASTER
   WHERE CLERNC IS NOT MISSING AND CLERNC < .50*ORIGINAL
   ORDER BY NAME;
```

STANDARD

```
PROC STANDARD DATA=SAS dataset OUT=SAS dataset options;
   VAR variables;
   optional statements
```

Standardizes numeric variables: converts them to a stated mean or standard deviation or replaces missing values with the mean value.

Options

MEAN or M=*number* Converts the variables to this mean.

STD or S=*number* Converts the variables to this standard deviation.

REPLACE Replaces missing values with mean values.

PRINT Prints the mean and standard deviation.

VARDEF=N or DF or WEIGHT or WGT or WDF

Statements

VAR *variables*; Standardizes these variables.

FREQ *variable*; The frequency variable.

WEIGHT *variable*; The weight variable.

Example

```
PROC STANDARD DATA=MODEL OUT=MMODEL REPLACE;
RUN;
```

SUMMARY

```
PROC SUMMARY DATA=SAS dataset options  statistics;
   optional statements
```

Computes descriptive statistics and frequencies of variables in a SAS dataset. The SUMMARY proc is essentially the same as the MEANS proc.

Options

PRINT Prints descriptive statistics. This is the default for the MEANS proc. NOPRINT Does not produce print output. This is the default for the SUMMARY proc.

MISSING Includes missing CLASS variable values.

NWAY Includes only the highest _TYPE_ value in the output.
DESCENDING Orders output by descending _TYPE_ value.

IDMIN Uses the minimum ID value, instead of the maximum.

FW=n The width of printed statistic values.

MAXDEC=n The maximum number of decimal places printed.

The order of output CLASS values: ORDER=DATA Order of appearance in the input data. ORDER=INTERNAL Sorted order. ORDER=EXTERNAL *or* FORMATTED Sorted order of the formatted values. ORDER=FREQ Descending order of frequency.

VARDEF=N *or* DF *or* WEIGHT *or* WGT *or* WDF

ALPHA=*confidence* Sets the confidence level used by the confidence level statistics LCLM and UCLM. **Release** 6.07+

Additional statistics LCLM UCLM **Release** 6.07+

Statements

CLASS *variables*; Forms groups according to the values of these variables.

ID *variables*; Also includes these variables in the output.

VAR *variables*; Computes statistics for these variables.

FREQ *variable*; The frequency variable.

WEIGHT *variable*; The weight variable.

OUTPUT OUT=*SAS dataset options*; Creates an output SAS dataset, with one observation for each combination of CLASS variable values.

OUTPUT statement options

statistic= Creates variables of this statistic for the VAR variables, with the same names.

statistic=*new variables* Creates variables of this statistic for the VAR variables, with the new names indicated.

statistic(*variables*)= Creates variables of this statistic for selected VAR variables, with the same names.

statistic(*variables*)=*new variables* Creates variables of this statistic for selected VAR variables, with the new names indicated.

MAXID(*variable* (ID *variables*) ...)=*new variables* Creates variables that show the value of ID variables in the observation that has the maximum value of the indicated VAR variable.

MINID(*variable* (ID *variables*) ...)=*new variables* Creates variables that show the value of ID variables in the observation that has the minimum value of the indicated VAR variable.

This step creates the SAS dataset CARTOTAL, with totals from the SAS dataset CAR:

```
PROC SUMMARY DATA=CARS NWAY;
  CLASS CAR;
  ID MAKE MODEL MODELYR;
  VAR MILEAGE DEPR;
  OUTPUT OUT=CARTOTAL SUM=;
RUN;
```

TABULATE

PROC TABULATE DATA=*SAS dataset options*;
  TABLE *request / options*; ...
  optional statements

Prints tables of descriptive statistics and frequencies of variables in a SAS dataset.

Options

DEPTH=*n* The maximum depth in any dimension. The default is DEPTH=10.

FORMAT=*format specification* The default format for cells. The default is FORMAT=12.2.

FORMCHAR(*index* ...)='*chars*' Overrides selected characters of the FORMCHAR= system option.

MISSING Includes missing CLASS variable values.

NOSEPS Suppresses horizontal rules.

The order of output CLASS values: ORDER=DATA Order of appearance in the input data. ORDER=INTERNAL Sorted order. ORDER=EXTERNAL *or* FORMATTED Sorted order of the formatted values. ORDER=FREQ Descending order of frequency.

VARDEF=N *or* DF *or* WEIGHT *or* WGT *or* WDF

Statements

CLASS *variables*; These variables define groups.

VAR *variables*; Analysis variables. Statistics are calculated for these variables.

KEYLABEL *statistic*='*label*' ...; Substitutes a label for a statistic name.

FREQ *variable*; The frequency variable.

WEIGHT *variable*; The weight variable.

TABLE *table expression / table options*; Defines the table.

Table expression

The columns, rows, and pages of a table are defined by a table expression, which consists of up to three dimension expressions that are separated by commas:

column expression
row expression, column expression
page expression, row expression, column expression

A dimension expression is made up of combinations of these elements:

class variable or ALL
analysis variable
statistic
F=*format specification*

='*label*'
(*element element* ...)
*element*x*element*

Joining two elements with an asterisk indicates that the elements are combined and form different levels in the table definition.

The dimension expressions are combined to form the table. The combination that forms any cell can include any number of class variables, but no more than one analysis variable, one statistic, and one format.

Statistics

PCTN⟨*denominator*⟩ A percent of a frequency.

PCTSUM⟨*denominator*⟩ A percent of a sum.

CSS CV MAX MEAN MAX MIN N NMISS PRT RANGE STD STDERR SUM SUMWGT USS T VAR

Table options

CONDENSE Combines pages within a BY group, when possible.

FUZZ=*number* Numbers closer to 0 than this number are treated as zero values.

MISSTEXT='*string*' Text printed for cells that contain missing values.

PRINTMISS Forms all combinations of CLASS variable values, even those that do not appear in the data.

ROW=CONSTANT *or* CONST Row title space is divided among all row levels. ROW=FLOAT Row title space is divided among nonblank title elements.

RTSPACE *or* RTS=*n* The size of the row title space.

BOX= The contents of the upper left corner box: '*string*' The string.
PAGE The page dimension text. *variable* The variable's name or label.

Example

```
 PROC TABULATE DATA=ELECTION MISSING;
   CLASS STATE CANDIDAT;
   VAR VOTES;
   TABLE STATE ALL,
      CANDIDAT*VOTES*(SUM*F=10. PCTSUM⟨STATE ALL⟩);
   LABEL CANDIDAT='CANDIDATE' VOTES='Votes';
   KEYLABEL SUM='Count' PCTSUM='Percent';
RUN;
```

TAPELABEL

```
 PROC TAPELABEL DDNAME=fileref;
```

Prints information from a standard tape label. **Operating system** MVS

TIMEPLOT

```
 PROC TIMEPLOT DATA=SAS dataset options;
   optional statements
   PLOT plot requests / plot options;
```

Plots variables in a sequence, with one row for each observation or group of observations.

Options

MAXDEC=*n* The maximum number of decimal positions to print.

UNIFORM   Uses the same horizontal scale for all BY groups.

Statements

CLASS *variables*;   Variables that define groups of observations. The input SAS dataset should be grouped by the class variables. Instead of printing one row for each observation, the PLOT statements print one row for each class group. If a symbol variable is not used, only the first observation in the class group is plotted.

ID *variables*;   Additional variables to be printed.

PLOT *plot requests / plot options*;   Defines one or more plots.

Plot requests

variable   The first character of the variable name is the plotting symbol.

variable or (variables) = *'symbol' or symbol variable*   The first nonblank character of the symbol constant or formatted symbol variable is the plotting symbol.

Plot options

AXIS=*value, value, ...*   AXIS=*start* TO *stop* BY *interval*   Defines the horizontal axis.

JOINREF   Connects the leftmost plotting or reference symbol in a line to the rightmost plotting or reference symbol with hyphens, unless the line does not contain any plotting symbols. HILOC   Connects the leftmost plotting symbol to the rightmost plotting symbol with hyphens.

NOSYMNAME   Does not print the name of the symbol variable if there is a CLASS statement.

NPP   Does not print the value of the plotted variables.

OVERLAY   Puts the entire PLOT statement on one plot.

OVPCHAR=*'char'*   The character that is printed when plotting symbols overlap. The default is OVPCHAR='@'.

POS=*n*   The plot width.

REF=*numbers*   Prints reference symbols at the points specified on each line. REF=MEAN(*variables*)   Prints reference symbols on each line at the point that represents the mean of each variable.

REFCHAR=*'symbol'*   The reference symbol. The default is REFCHAR='|'.

REVERSE   Arranges the axis in descending order.

TRANSPOSE

PROC TRANSPOSE DATA=*SAS dataset* OUT=*SAS dataset* *options*;
optional statements

Transposes: converts observations to variables and variables to observations. If you use a BY statement, BY groups are transposed separately.

Options

PREFIX=*prefix*   The prefix that is used to create output variables names if you do not use an ID statement.

LET   Allows duplicate ID values.

NAME=*variable*   The name for the output variable that contains the input variable names. The default is NAME=_NAME_.

LABEL=*variable* The name for the output variable that contains the input variable labels. The default is LABEL=_LABEL_.

Statements

VAR *variables*; These variables are transposed. By default, numeric variables not named in other statements are transposed.

COPY *variables*; These variables are copied without transposing.

ID *variable*; The input variable that is used to form output variable names.

IDLABEL *or* IDL *variable*; The input variable that is used to form output variable labels.

Examples

This step converts the variable TEMP to a separate variable for each different value of MONTH in the input SAS dataset:

```
  PROC TRANSPOSE DATA=AREATEMP OUT=AREAMON;
    BY TOWN;
    ID MONTH;
    VAR TEMP;
RUN;
```

If there is only one observation in each BY group in the SAS dataset AREAMON, the step below converts the numeric variables in that SAS dataset to the variable TEMP1. The number of output observations per BY group is determined by the number of numeric variables.

```
  PROC TRANSPOSE DATA=AREAMON OUT=AREATOWN
    NAME=MONTH PREFIX=TEMP;
    BY TOWN;
RUN;
```

TRANTAB

```
  PROC TRANTAB TABLE=name option;
    optional statements
```

Loads a translation table for editing. **Release** 6.07+ RUN

Option

NLS Loads one of the SAS System internal translation tables: SASXPT, SASLCL, SASUCS, SASLCS, or SASCCL.

Statements

LIST *area option*; Writes the translation table in the log, using hexadecimal notation.

CLEAR *area option*; Sets all positions in the translation table to zero.

REPLACE *position value(s)*; Sets position(s) in the translation table, beginning at the indicated position, with the indicated value(s). The position can be a number from 0 to 255 or a character. The values can be numbers from 0 to 255, characters, and/or character strings.

INVERSE; Inverts area one, the device-to-host area of the translation table, to create area two, the host-to-device area of the translation table.

SWAP; Exchanges areas one and two of the translation table. To edit area two, use the SWAP statement, one or more REPLACE statements, and another SWAP statement.

SAVE TABLE=*entry area option*; Stores the edited translation table as a catalog entry of type TRANTAB.

LOAD TABLE=*name option*; Loads a different translation table for editing.
Option NLS

Area options ONE Area one; the device-to-host area of the translation table. TWO Area two; the host-to-device area of the translation table. BOTH Both areas.

UNIVARIATE
PROC UNIVARIATE DATA=*SAS dataset options*;
  optional statements
Computes statistics for variables.

Options
NOPRINT Suppresses all print output.

FREQ Prints a frequency table.

NORMAL Tests the hypothesis that the input data is normally distributed.

PCTLDEF=1 *or* 2 *or* 3 *or* 4 *or* 5 Methods for calculating percentiles.

PLOT Produces plots.

ROUND=*number*... Variable values are rounded before processing. Use either one roundoff number or a separate one for each variable in the VAR statement.

VARDEF=N *or* DF *or* WEIGHT *or* WGT *or* WDF

Statements
VAR *variables*; Analysis variables. Statistics are computed for these variables.

ID *variables*; Additional variables that are copied to the output SAS dataset and printed for the smallest and largest observations.

FREQ *variable*; The frequency variable.

WEIGHT *variable*; The weight variable.

OUTPUT OUT=*SAS dataset options*; Defines an output SAS dataset.

OUTPUT statement options
statistic=*variables* Names output variables that contain the indicated statistic for the analysis variables. Provide one variable name for each analysis variable. In addition to the usual statistics, these statistics can be used: MEDIAN Q1 Q3 QRANGE P1 P5 P10 P90 P95 P99 MODE MSIGN PROBM SIGNRANK PROBS NORMAL PROBN

PCTLPTC=*n*... $0 \le n \le 100$ Creates variables that contain the indicated percentiles for the analysis variables.

PCTLPRE=*prefixes* Defines prefixes used to create variable names for percentiles. Provide one prefix for each analysis variable.

PCTLNAME=*suffixes* Defines suffixes used in place of the percentile numbers to create variable names for percentiles.

V5TOV6

PROC V5TOV6 IN=*libref or* FORMAT=SASLIB OUT=*libref options*; *optional statements*

Converts a SAS version 5 data library or format library to a SAS version 6 library. **Operating system** Multiuser **Release** 6.06+

Options

ENTRYTYPE *or* ETYPE *or* ET=(*v. 5 entry types*)

MEMTYPE *or* MTYPE *or* MT=(*v. 5 member types*)

LIST Lists files, but does not convert them.

READ=*password* **Release** 6.06 only

Statements

SELECT *or* EXCLUDE *member* (*options*) ... / *options*; Copies selected members. **Options** MT=*v. 5 member type* READ=*password*

CAT SELECT *or* EXCLUDE *catalog.entry* (*option*) ... / *option*; Selects screen catalog entries. You can use both CAT SELECT and CAT EXCLUDE statements as long as you do not name any one catalog in both statements. **Option** ET=*v. 5 entry type*

GCAT SELECT *or* EXCLUDE *catalog.entry* ... ; Selects graphics catalog entries. You can use both GCAT SELECT and GCAT EXCLUDE statements as long as you do not name any one catalog in both statements.

XCOPY

PROC XCOPY IN=*libref* OUT=*fileref* EXPORT
       or IN=*fileref* OUT=*libref* IMPORT;
optional statement

Exports or imports a transport file that contains SAS datasets. **Operating system** MVS, CMS

Statements

SELECT *SAS datasets*; *or* EXCLUDE *SAS datasets*; Copies selected SAS datasets.

19
Products

The SAS System is made up of a set of products. Each product can be licensed separately. Most products consist mainly of a set of procs; others are interactive applications.

Base SAS

Base SAS software is the essential product of the SAS System. It includes the supervisor, informats, formats, functions, and CALL routines. It also includes utility, reporting, and analytic procs.

SAS/AF

With SAS/AF software, you can create user interfaces and interactive applications that work with the SAS System. **Proc** BUILD

SAS/ETS

SAS/ETS software is a set of procs for econometrics, time series analysis, and financial applications. **Procs** ARIMA AUTOREG CITIBASE COMPUTAB EXPAND FORECAST LOAN MODEL MORTGAGE PDLREG SIMLIN SPECTRA STATESPACE SYSLIN TSCSREG X11

SAS/FSP

SAS/FSP software is a collection of interactive procs for working with SAS datasets and text data. **Procs** FSBROWSE FSEDIT FSLETTER FSLIST FSVIEW

SAS/GRAPH

SAS/GRAPH software creates graphs and maps and works with graphical objects. It includes a drawing program. It also includes a set of routines that can be used in data steps to create graphical objects. **Procs** G3D G3GRID GANNO GCHART GCONTOUR GDEVICE GFONT GIMPORT GKEYMAP GMAP GOPTIONS GPLOT GPRINT GPROJECT GREDUCE GREMOVE GREPLAY GSLIDE GTESTIT

SAS/OR

SAS/OR software analyzes operations research problems, including networks and project scheduling, and does linear programming. **Procs** ASSIGN CPM DTREE GANTT LP NETDRAW NETFLOW NLP TRANS

SAS/QC

SAS/QC software contains procs for quality reporting, analysis, and control. **Procs** CAPABILITY CUSUM FACTEX ISHIKAWA MACONTROL OPTEX PARETO SHEWHART

SAS/STAT

SAS/STAT software implements statistical tests, analyses, and reports. **Procs** ACECLUS ANOVA CALIS CANCORR CANDISC CATMOD CLUSTER CORRESP DISCRIM FACTOR FASTCLUS GLM INBREED LATTICE LIFEREG LIFETEST LOGISTIC MDS MIXED MULTTEST NESTED NLIN NPAR1WAY ORTHOREG PHREG PLAN PRINCOMP PRINQUAL PROBIT REG RSREG SCORE STEPDISC TRANSREG TREE TTEST VARCLUS VARCOMP

Other products

SAS/ACCESS   SAS data views for direct access to database and other file formats. **Release** 6.06+

SAS/ASSIST   Interactive menu-driven interface for the SAS System. **Release** 6.06+

SAS/CALC   A 3-D spreadsheet program with 3-D graphics.

SAS/CONNECT   Links SAS sessions on separate computers.

SAS/CPE   Computer performance evaluation. **Operating system** VMS

SAS/EIS   Object-oriented user interfaces. **Release** 6.08+

SAS/ENGLISH   Natural-language interface. **Release** 6.08+

SAS/GRAPH+   A new look for SAS/GRAPH graphics. **Release** 6.08+

SAS/IML   Matrix processing.

SAS/INSIGHT   Exploratory data analysis with 3-D graphics. **Release** 6.07+

SAS/LAB   Guidance for routine statistical analysis. **Release** 6.07+

SAS/NVISION   High-resolution 3-D color graphics and animation. **Release** 6.08+

SAS/PH-Clinical   Clinical trials of experimental drugs. **Operating system** Multiuser **Release** 6.07+

SAS/SHARE   Simultaneous access to SAS files. **Operating system** Multiuser **Release** 6.07+

Index